Harry Potter

WIZARDS OF BAKING

THE OFFICIAL
COMPANION GUIDE

Harry Potter

WIZARDS OF BAKING

THE OFFICIAL
COMPANION GUIDE

Recipes by Zoë Burmester, Jordan Pilarski,
Gabriella English, Elena P. Craig, and Sarah Walker Caron
Additional material by Richard Mead

INSIGHT
EDITIONS

SAN RAFAEL · LOS ANGELES · LONDON

TASK 1 PLATFORM 9¾

TASK 2 GRINGOTTS

TASK 3 DIAGON ALLEY

TASK 4 FORBIDDEN FOREST

TASK 5 DUMBLEDORE'S OFFICE

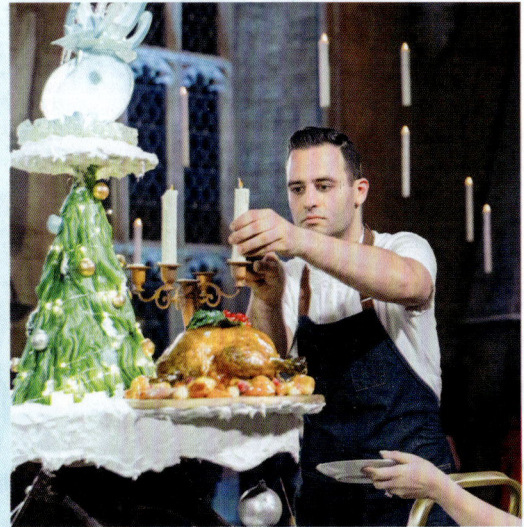

TASK 6 THE GREAT HALL

CONTENTS

---✳---

✴

FOREWORD

BY ZOË AND JORDAN, WINNERS

✳

"**F**ood is a language that is universal. As chefs, being able to speak that language and share it with others is a massive motivator for both of us. And being able to combine it with the world of Harry Potter was a fantastic opportunity. *Wizards of Baking* was so much more than a regular baking show. Being invited to the Warner Bros. Studio Tour in Leavesden, UK, with the Harry Potter actors on set, came with a big responsibility because those films are so adored. The competition proved to be one of the hardest things we have ever done, but to be standing in the Great Hall at the end and realize what we had just accomplished was an incredible feeling that we will never forget."

"When I applied for *Wizards of Baking*, I was hoping to be paired with somebody who was levelheaded, honest, and a hard worker. Also, I hoped it would be someone I could communicate with freely, without fear of upsetting egos. I knew that the standard of everybody on the show was going to be high, so it was never a question of people's ability. For me, it was very much about personality type, and the second I spoke to Jordan, I knew that I'd lucked out!

Harry Potter is an iconic franchise, and we wanted to play our part in that. It definitely added a dimension that other shows we have participated in didn't have. It was such a unique experience for Jordan and me to create intricately layered but large and impactful showpieces for such an iconic story. It was important to us that we not only storytell visually with the piece but also within the flavors themselves. We genuinely collaborated on every single flavor profile, and I'm really proud of us for that. We had never worked together before, and we bring different skills to the challenges. Jordan is way more experienced in certain disciplines, but I also have a lot of culinary and artistic experience. Being British, like Hogwarts and Harry, I felt it was important to bring those flavors and successfully combine them with Jordan's influences. I think we achieved that!"

ZOË BURMESTER

"I'm a happy person, and I wanted a teammate that I could get along with, enjoy the experience together, and leave the show as friends. I feel like Zoë and I are now friends for life. We have been through so much just in that short amount of time. I feel that a lot of people don't understand what it's like to be in these situations. You learn a lot about each other. Zoë is an amazing cake artist and extremely creative, but then you start to learn about her family, and where she's from, and who she is as a person. If you don't get along, that makes it very difficult. It felt a bit like speed dating!

Happily, Zoë and I were on the same page throughout every process, and it made the experience a lot less stressful. We had fun at every point of the competition, and that was important. We both laughed and we made each other laugh.

We had an open line of communication from the beginning. There was a lot of talk about certain things—and flavor was huge. I knew from personal experience that the showpieces needed to look amazing, but our tasting elements needed to blow the judges out of the water. The judges are going to critique the builds, but when they start eating things, that's a different level of competition. You can make anything look great, but if it doesn't taste good ... that's it!"

JORDAN PILARSKI

The
TEAMS

The eighteen chefs demonstrating their spectacular skills on *Wizards of Baking* all applied to the show individually. They were then organized into nine pairs by the production team—hopefully, the Sorting Hat would have approved! The bakers' success in the competition would partly depend on how well they worked together, dividing up the tasks to ensure that each chef's particular strengths were being utilized to the utmost. It meant the contest would be a challenge of communication and cooperation, as much as culinary proficiency. For the newly formed baking partnerships, teamwork would prove vital to conjuring up some kitchen magic.

ZOË & JORDAN

Both proud Hufflepuffs, Zoë and Jordan embody the house traits
of patience and dedication—and Helga Hufflepuff's love of food.

Zoë

**CAKE ARTIST AND OWNER OF
SUGAR STREET STUDIOS**

Originally from London, Zoë Burmester now
lives in Brooklyn, New York. A self-taught baker
and natural artist, she is adept in sculpted
creations, whether they are cakes, cookies,
or cake pops.

> ## "I've never made
> ### the same cake twice."

Zoë loves attempting cake designs that
haven't been done before. Imaginative,
super-realistic cakes are her specialty, and she
loves sculpting animals. Her attention to detail
and strong sense of storytelling has led to many
accolades. Named as one of the UK's Top 10
Cake Artists in 2019, she is a previous champion
on Food Network and a five-time winner at
Cake International.

Her first introduction to the world of Harry
Potter was visiting the set of the first movie.
As a cake artist, she is particularly inspired by
the amazing creatures, as well as the theme
of food that is peppered throughout the films.

Jordan

**EXECUTIVE PASTRY CHEF AT
OJAI VALLEY INN AND SPA**

Jordan Pilarski originally planned to follow in
the footsteps of his grandfather, an architect,
until he developed an interest in baking. Now,
he uses his precise, meticulous mind to create
aesthetically pleasing, detailed desserts.

After graduating with a bachelor of arts
degree from Johnson & Wales University
in Providence, Rhode Island, Jordan began
his career working at five-star hotels. He
subsequently used his baking skills to win
multiple Food Network competitions.

Jordan likens himself to a house-elf
who works in the kitchen, before magically
transporting his plated desserts to the guests
in the Great Hall! However, he recognizes he
also has a Slytherin-style competitive streak.
Jordan has a long-standing ambition to make
a Polyjuice Potion dessert in an edible tube
that releases smoke when opened.

> ### "Pastry school was
> ## magic school for me."

HEMU & RICCARDO

These two chefs are joining forces to combine their amazing technical skills—with their wicked senses of humor!

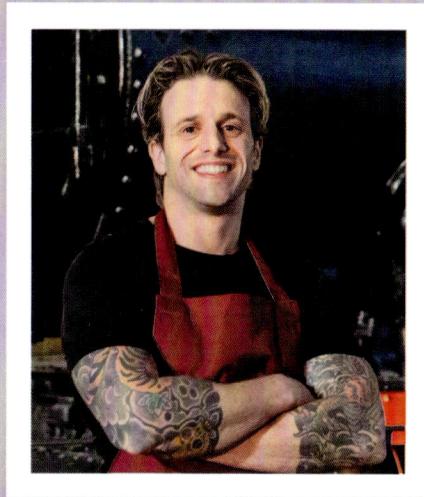

Hemu

CAKE ARTIST AND OWNER OF HEMU'S SWEET SENSATION

"I create the most amazing cakes you have ever seen!"

Indian American cake artist Hemu Basumatary began her baking adventure in 2012, when her son asked her to make him a fire truck cake. Teaching herself from library books, she has risen to the top of her field.

Hemu has a talent for turning everyday objects into edible masterpieces—she once created a six-foot-tall phonograph cake, which looked identical to the real thing. Her work has been featured in major publications, and she has won multiple cake competitions, including *The Big Bake* on Food Network in 2022.

A self-confessed movie fan, her favorite film is *Harry Potter and the Sorcerer's Stone*. She also confesses that she has a soft spot for Dobby, because he is loyal to Harry and his friends. She would like to bake a cake for the house-elf that looks like a stack of clothes, flavored with vanilla, funfetti, and chocolate.

Riccardo

EXECUTIVE PASTRY CHEF AT BEVERLY WILSHIRE, A FOUR SEASONS HOTEL

Born in Florence, Italy, Riccardo Menicucci grew up in a family full of fashion designers and chefs. After attending art school to hone his skills in sculpting and painting, he pursued his passion of creating edible art with pastries.

Riccardo began working aged seventeen, before moving to San Francisco to become executive pastry chef for Acquerello, a two-star Michelin restaurant. He enjoys the chemical and mathematical approach to the laws of pastry and is always ready to try something new.

"When people see my desserts, I want them to say, 'Wow!'"

He was once given just five hours' notice to create a Sorting Hat dessert packed with macarons for a hotel guest, who was a Harry Potter fan. Riccardo would love to make a life-size Dementor out of chocolate, with a wispy cloak and bony hands!

KAYLA & YOHANN

The Harry Potter films evoke many joyful family memories for Kayla and Yohann, providing inspiration for their breathtaking bakes.

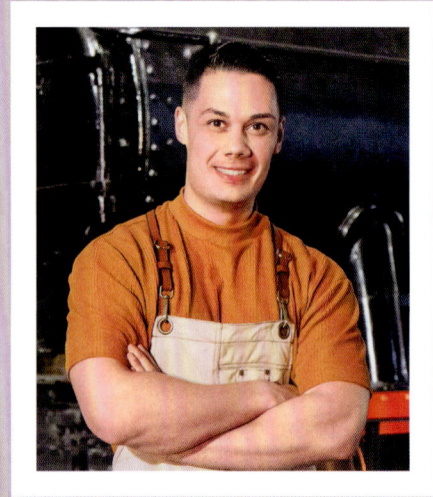

Kayla

CAKE DESIGNER AND OWNER OF CHEERS TO CAKE

Kayla Giddings describes her specialty as being able to create realistic things out of cake, be it a car, crown, or creature. She attributes her success to saying yes to everything.

> ## "I really like flavors
> ### that I grew up with."

The clever cake artist from Lafayette loves to infuse her Louisiana pride into the flavors and textures of her imaginative designs. Kayla's favorite creation is her take on the Mardi Gras King cake. Her version is a dense red velvet cake filled with praline pieces and a flavor-packed frosting. She has won TV shows, such as *Cake Wars* and *Food Network Challenge*.

Kayla has been obsessed with Harry Potter and Hogwarts since she was eleven and now shares her love of the movies with her daughter. She loves how the film series reveals new, magical candies and dreams of bringing the Hogwarts Express food trolley to life through cake.

Yohann

EXECUTIVE PASTRY CHEF AT WORLD EQUESTRIAN CENTER

Yohann Le Bescond loves the technical precision that baking requires. He wants every element of his desserts to be flawless.

When he was fifteen, Yohann started his first job in a pastry shop before participating in an apprenticeship program. He graduated summa cum laude with the esteemed Brevet Technique des Métiers Pâtissier, the highest trade certification in France. Restaurant Hospitality named him on their 2023 Power List of notable chefs around the world.

Growing up, Yohann would pretend to be Hermione Granger and yell, "*Wingardium Leviosa*," while waving a wand. He would like to create a dessert based around the Battle of Hogwarts, with a castle-shaped cake surrounded by a large sugar dome.

> ## "One of my **biggest**
> ### **inspirations** is nature
> ## and real fruits."

CONNER & MICHAEL

This union of prodigy and pro has a softer side—the talented pair are drawn to the theme of love in the Harry Potter films.

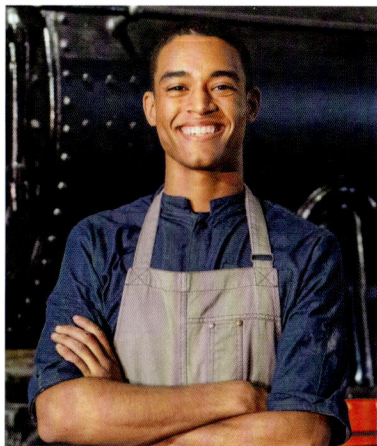

Conner

**PASTRY CHEF AT
THE HYATT TEXAS**

The youngest competitor, Conner Strackman is a standout pastry talent from Smithville, Texas. His open-minded approach allows him to think outside the box, experimenting freely with his style.

> "Watch out, because I know
> **exactly what I'm doing**
> in the kitchen."

Conner is the youngest graduate from Amaury Guichon's esteemed Pastry Academy. Currently working at Hyatt Regency Lost Pines, he plans to advance his pastry skills in Paris soon. When off-duty, Conner engages his followers on Instagram with his culinary experiments.

The young chef believes that if he were a student at Hogwarts, his best friend would be Hermione. He describes the Gryffindor pupil as being smart and courageous but with an unexpected bite to her, which applies to Conner, too.

Michael

**PASTRY CHEF AND OWNER OF
MACDADDY OAKLAND**

Michael Russ II is not one to shy away from a challenge. After graduating from his baking and pastry program with four degrees with high honors, he decided to take on Las Vegas, one of the most demanding cities for pastry.

Baking for celebrities doesn't faze Michael; his creations have been sampled by Britney Spears and Jennifer Lopez. Martha Stewart told Michael that his baking was "delicious."

Michael's love for Harry Potter began when his grandmother bought him the books as a child. He treasures these gifts because his grandmother signed each one of them with love before she passed away. He also collected the Harry Potter LEGO® sets—and believed that his letter inviting him to study at Hogwarts had been lost in the mail!

> "I am definitely a
> **culinary wizard.**"

LISA & MITZI

With shared Mexican heritage, a preference for being quirky,
and dazzling culinary prowess, Lisa and Mitzi make a model match.

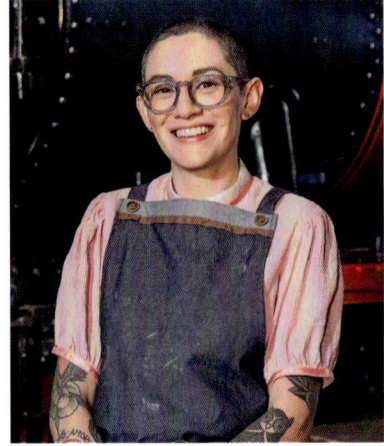

Lisa

EXECUTIVE CHEF AND OWNER OF
A REAL SWEET THING

Lisa Altfest discovered her skill and love for baking at a young age. She has since become a world-renowned cake artist, wowing clients with her incredible edible creations.

> "I am mostly known for the cakes that you walk by **without realizing it's a cake.**"

After training in confectionery arts, Lisa was diagnosed with celiac disease and has since perfected gluten-free creations for the biggest sweet tooth! The largest cake she has ever made was her own massive nine-tier wedding cake. Lisa believes that you could have walked around it for an hour—and still not experienced all of its hidden treasures!

Lisa is a passionate super-fan of the Harry Potter series. She is a proud member of Hufflepuff house and names her Hufflepuff sweater as her most prized possession. She laments that her husband is "pure Muggle."

Mitzi

EXECUTIVE PASTRY CHEF AT
THE CURTIS STONE GROUP

Mitzi Reyes grew up in Mexico City and discovered her passion for cooking by helping her grandfather, who was a chef, in the kitchen.

Mitzi graduated from Le Cordon Bleu, where she studied both savory and pastry, in 2008. She has worked under Michelin Star–chefs José Andrés and Dominique Ansel. Mitzi loves creating elevated desserts, including her current favorite dish, which is a mojito-flavored dessert that resembles a lime.

The Harry Potter films are special to her because her father took Mitzi and her sister to see them at the cinema. Unfortunately, he has now passed, and watching the movies rekindles a lot of fond memories for her. She can't wait until her daughter is old enough for them to both enjoy the films together.

> "I think my imagination has no limits; **I like to challenge my brain.**"

JESS & JAMIE

Family provides motivation for both Jess and Jamie's baking success and is a theme that resonates with them in the wizarding world.

Jess

EXECUTIVE PASTRY CHEF AND OWNER OF PIPED PASTRY SHOP

For the past twenty-five years, Jess Lewis has called Washington, D.C., home, where she is renowned as one of the country's top pastry chefs with her skilled dessert creations.

"I love being a pastry chef; I love making desserts."

After attending the culinary program at the Art Institute of Washington, Jess began her career at Windows Catering Company under fourteen-time gold medal pastry chef Laurent Lhuillier. As the pastry sous chef at Fiola Mare, she further refined her craft, having the opportunity to plate desserts for President Barack Obama and other political figures.

Jess watched her first Harry Potter movie in her twenties and was hooked. She reckons that she is part Gryffindor and part Hufflepuff. The film character she identifies with most is Ron Weasley because she says they are both "quirky, funny, and slightly immature."

Jamie

PASTRY CHEF AND OWNER OF SUGARNOVA

Growing up in Southern California, Jamie Louks always felt that she was the "weird" kid. Her parents used to joke that it would be great to have a chef in the family, which motivated Jamie to begin her culinary career.

After working in hotels, catering companies, and high-end restaurants, Jamie started her own business. She prides herself on making her bakes unusual and unique and takes inspiration from what she might find in curiosity shops or antique stores. A passion for competition has earned her the title of *Baketopia* champion.

Jamie became a Harry Potter fan when she read the novels as a middle school student. She is enjoying watching the movies again with her two daughters, but only after they've read the relevant book first!

"Baking is that perfect balance of being an artist and being a scientist at the same time."

ASHLEY & KIMBERLY

Discovering their passion for baking at an early age, both Ashley and Kimberly are experts in conjuring up sculpted cakes.

Ashley

EXECUTIVE PASTRY CHEF AT CIRCA 1886, WENTWORTH MANSION

Ashley Cardona's journey has taken her from assisting her grandmother in the kitchen during summer breaks to becoming an accomplished and classically trained pastry chef known for her showstopping centerpieces.

"I am passionate about pastry."

Ashley's specialties include large-scale gingerbread constructions and intricate chocolate sculptures. For a Halloween dessert special, she took inspiration from the Forbidden Forest and made a realistic-looking pumpkin under a smoke-filled cloche, which released an applewood bouquet when the lid was raised.

Ashley is a Ravenclaw and says she exhibits the house traits of being an independent thinker, being creative, and having a thirst for knowledge. As a firm Mrs. Weasley fan, she would love to learn all the mom hacks she must have discovered after raising seven children!

Kimberly

OWNER AND CEO OF SIGNATURE SWEETS BAKERY

Born and raised in Milwaukee, Kimberly Adams found her calling when she was growing up, following her mother, who baked from scratch.

Although initially teaching herself, Kimberly is also a graduate of the prestigious Le Cordon Bleu program. She is renowned for her larger-than-life structured cakes that evoke emotions with their artistic designs. She is proud of an eight-tier wedding cake that she created; the tiers were round and square and each had a different flavor. When she's not in the kitchen, Kimberly travels the world with her family.

Kimberly would love to immortalize Hedwig in cake, on an isomalt tree with leaves made from crunchy wafer paper. She thinks she and Hermione would be great friends because they are both "smart know-it-alls!"

"My cakes do the absolute most—they smoke, they light up, they spin."

MIKO & CHRIS

These skilled chefs share a secret—although they were placed in other houses by the Sorting Hat, they reckon they are both Slytherins!

Miko

**FREELANCE
CAKE DECORATOR/ARTIST**

New York–based Miko Kaw Hok Uy majored in painting, and his passion for art is evident in his beautifully designed illusion cakes. It's difficult not to believe that sorcery is involved when looking at his amazing creations!

> "Honestly, my kind of fun is staying at **home and working on cakes.**"

Miko likes to think outside the box when working on a commission. The *New York Times* contacted him to make an edible display to accompany a magazine feature. Miko created a platter of fruit on a board, but no one would believe it was all made from cake, until he cut into a "pear" to reveal the icing.

Miko uses the Harry Potter films to relieve stress and will happily watch all the movies in order from the first to the last. His favorite villains include Lord Voldemort and Professor Dolores Umbridge because they stir the pot!

Chris

**EXECUTIVE PASTRY CHEF AT
FIFTY/50 RESTAURANT GROUP**

Award-winning pastry chef Chris Teixeira was born in Portugal but is now based in Chicago. His dishes bring European flair combined with Midwestern work ethic.

Chris is known for chocolate showpieces that engage all the senses with unexpected flavors, sights, and sounds. He has created desserts that are enveloped in smoke or fire or create a sound when eaten. In 2019, Chris passed the Certified Master Baker examination through the Retail Bakers of America—this is the highest certification available.

Chris read his first Harry Potter book in sixth grade—and still has that copy today. He says that he has been compared to a Death Eater many times and would like to meet Lucius Malfoy. He explains: "I would probably hang out with that kind of group. Not to say that I want to take over the world, but they seem kind of cool!"

> "If you're not coming to **win,** then don't come at all."

ELIZABETH & JUAN

When they were children, accomplished bakers Elizabeth and Juan found comfort and creativity in the wizarding world.

Elizabeth

CAKE ARTIST AND OWNER OF THE LONDON BAKER

Elizabeth Rowe discovered her love for edible art when she was twenty-one. After her first session in the kitchen, the British-born baker was hooked on experimenting with flavors and recipes.

> ## "It needs to taste
> ### as good as it looks."

Elizabeth is entirely self-taught. Her skills in the kitchen, which include isomalt, fondant, and royal icing, were learned through years of trial and error. She runs two Texas bakeries, and her name has become synonymous with hyper-realistic pop culture cakes.

Every room in Elizabeth's house has a touch of the wizarding world, including blue Cornish Pixie figurines and her DIY Dobby statue. Every few months, she hosts a Harry Potter high tea at a local restaurant. She is a Gryffindor—one test she took sorted her into Hufflepuff, but Elizabeth reckons that was a glitch!

Juan

EXECUTIVE PASTRY CHEF AT THE ST. REGIS CHICAGO

Growing up in a small city in Colombia, Juan Gutierrez thought he was going to be a doctor, like many of his family. After one semester at medical school, he knew that was not his dream—and realized he had a passion for food instead. At age eighteen, he moved to Chicago to pursue a career in pastry.

Juan particularly enjoys working with chocolate and loves to wow with his classic showpieces. Using nostalgic flavors, he aims to create dishes that will spark memories in his patrons while they eat his desserts. He also travels the globe, teaching his techniques.

Juan watched the Harry Potter movies with his brother. They would then pretend they were wizards, casting the *Petrificus Totalus* curse on each other! Juan would love to invent a magic potion that changes how diners taste his dishes.

> ## "I am one of the best chocolatiers, not only in Chicago, but also the world."

BAKING WIZARD: EQUIPMENT

The show's bakers were able to utilize specialist equipment—a diffuser spray booth, anyone?—but their core kit was a little more down-to-earth.

CAKE BOARDS

Lightweight boards used to create stability and structure between layers in a cake, helping to prevent them from sinking or being wonky. This is particularly useful in cakes with many layers or for particularly dense cakes.

CAKE-DECORATING TURNTABLE

Useful for positioning your undecorated cakes on, as you can rotate it while you decorate the sides and top with buttercream, frosting, or other decorations.

CAKE PANS

Round or square metallic tins that come in a variety of sizes. Springform cake pans have a separate base and sides held together with an interlocking band that can be released once the cake is done, which makes removing it from the tin much easier and allows it to cool more quickly.

COOKIE SHEET/FLAT BAKING SHEET

A flat baking tray with no edges, except with one small rim to hold on to, while getting it in and out of the oven. These are great for baking things made from a thicker batter, such as cookies, as the mixture will not run off the sides during baking, and, as there are no high sides, the heat can penetrate all around to ensure even baking.

CUTTERS

Usually made from metal or plastic, these are used to shape biscuit dough before baking or cut shapes out of cakes once they are baked.

FOOD PROCESSOR

An electric appliance with interchangeable blades and a lid that locks into place, used to finely chop or purée the contents inside it.

HAND MIXER

A smaller handheld device with two smaller whisk attachments, used to cream together butter and sugar for cake mixtures and buttercream and for whipping egg whites and cream.

OFFSET SPATULA

Also known as an angled palette knife, this is a kitchen tool with a bend near the handle and a thin, rounded metal blade. It is used for tasks such as spreading icing and frosting over cakes and spreading batter to the corners of pans.

PARCHMENT PAPER

Nonstick, greaseproof, and heat-resistant paper used extensively for baking and cooking. It is perfect for lining cake pans and cookie sheets, ensuring that your baked goods don't stick to the trays.

PARING KNIFE

A small, sharp knife used for cutting and carving when delicacy is needed, for example, when cutting pastry or fondant.

PASTRY BAG/PIPING BAG

Either disposable or reusable, made from plastic, nylon, silicone, or cotton. This is used to squeeze out soft food mixtures, such as buttercream, frosting, batter, and whipped cream. It can come with a hole at the narrow end or you can cut your own, and you can insert a nozzle to create specific patterns and shapes. Often used to decorate cakes and can be used to write words and messages on baked goods.

RAMEKINS

Small dishes, often made of ceramic or glass, that are used to contain individual desserts, such as crème brûlée or mousse.

ROLLING PIN

A cylindrical tool used for rolling out pastry, dough, or fondant icing, to flatten or shape it evenly.

SERRATED KNIFE

Serrated knives have sharp, scalloped edges, which make them perfect for slicing bread or leveling the surface of a cake, to shape it before decorating.

SILICONE BAKING MAT

Silicone baking mats are used at high temperatures in the oven and low ones in the freezer. They are very helpful in baking because you can easily roll dough out on them and then take them from prep station to chilling to oven, without having to move your dough. They are extremely nonstick and easy to clean.

STAND MIXER

A heavy-duty machine with a stand that a mixing bowl fits into, with various attachments, such as a flat paddle for beating together butter and sugar and making thicker batters, a whisk attachment for whipping egg whites and cream, and dough hooks for kneading doughs.

WIRE RACK

A slightly raised rectangular wire structure designed to keep hot pans and baked goods from touching your work surface while allowing air to circulate, enabling them to cool evenly.

BAKING WIZARD: INGREDIENTS

Stock up on the right basic ingredients, and you could make magic of your own in the kitchen.

ALL-PURPOSE FLOUR

Also known as plain flour, this is a finely ground flour without the addition of any rising agents, such as baking powder or bicarbonate of soda. It is commonly used to make cakes, pastries, and biscuits, as well as a huge range of other recipes.

BAKING POWDER

This is a dry leavening agent that is used to simultaneously lighten the texture and increase the volume of baked goods. It is inactive until it is mixed with a liquid, so to ensure your baked goods have the best outcome, you should try to get them in the oven as quickly as possible after combining wet and dry ingredients.

BAKING SODA

Similar to baking powder, baking soda is a dry leavening agent. Naturally alkaline, it reacts particularly well when used with acidic ingredients, such as citrus, or with soured dairy products, such as yogurt, buttermilk, or sour cream.

CACAO NIBS

Small pieces of crushed cacao beans with a bitter and strong chocolate flavor.

COCOA POWDER

An unsweetened chocolate product that adds a rich chocolate flavor to recipes. It is created when cocoa butter is removed from cacao beans while they are being processed.

COCONUT OIL

An oil taken from the kernels, flesh, and milk of coconuts that is a solid fat until heated. It adds a subtle coconut flavor and can be used in a variety of sweet and savory recipes.

DARK CHOCOLATE

A type of chocolate that contains a high percentage of cocoa and cocoa butter. It often contains little to no milk and is ideal in baking, as it adds a really strong chocolate flavor.

DESICCATED COCONUT

Taken from the flesh of the coconut, then dried, then finely grated. It can be used in both sweet and savory recipes.

EGGS

An incredibly useful ingredient, as they bind ingredients together, add structure to baked goods, thicken sauces and custards, work as a leavening agent, add moisture, and can be brushed onto pastry and bread before baking. They really are magic! Large eggs are generally used in baking. Always use room temperature eggs when making cake batters, as this will make it less likely that the mixture will split.

FOOD COLORING

Edible dye used to color food. It generally comes in liquid or gel form, with the gel being a lot more intense, usually meaning a little goes a long way.

GELATIN

An almost colorless and tasteless thickening agent made from collagen, making it unsuitable for vegans or vegetarians, though specifically vegetarian types are available. It is water-soluble and comes in leaf and powder forms.

GRANULATED SUGAR

A coarse white sugar that is often used in baking and to make sugar syrups or caramels, due to its surface area being larger than superfine, which makes crystallization less likely.

HEAVY CREAM

Thick dairy cream with a high fat content. Can be used in baking and savory cooking. Its higher fat content means that it is suitable for cooking, as it doesn't split when heated.

KOSHER SALT

Coarse-grained and unrefined type of salt used in cooking and baking to add a lovely crunch with a pure salty tang.

LIGHT BROWN SUGAR

Made by mixing white sugar with molasses, giving it a deep caramel color and flavor and higher moisture content.

LIGHT OLIVE OIL

A type of olive oil that has been refined to have a lighter color and more neutral flavor than less refined types of olive oil. It is ideal for use in cooking, as less refined types of olive oil can turn bitter during heating.

LUSTER DUST

This dust is a food-safe glitter that can be purchased online or in specialty baking stores. It can be mixed with clear alcohol to create a shimmery paint or brushed on dry.

POWDERED SUGAR

Also known as icing sugar or confectioners' sugar, this baking essential is made by milling granulated sugar to a powdered state. It is used to make icing, such as buttercream, or frostings, such as cream cheese frosting. It is also sieved over baked goods as decoration and to add additional sweetness.

SELF-RISING FLOUR

An all-purpose flour with the addition of baking powder and salt, making it a great staple in baking recipes. In some recipes, you will need to add extra baking powder or baking soda with it to ensure the mixture rises and cooks through properly.

SUPERFINE SUGAR

Granulated sugar that has been ground into finer crystals. It is often used for baking cakes and meringues and for stabilizing beaten egg whites due to its ability to dissolve more quickly.

UNSALTED BUTTER

Pure butter with no added salt. It is ideal for baking, as you can control the amount of salt in your bakes by either leaving it out completely or adding a pinch if needed.

VANILLA EXTRACT

Made by the process of macerating vanilla pods in a mixture of ethanol and water. It has a natural sweetness that complements many baked goods and is used in a wide variety of baking recipes to add extra flavor.

Vanilla Paste vs. Vanilla Extract

Vanilla bean paste can give you the strong vanilla flavor and the beautiful vanilla bean flecks without having to split and steep a vanilla bean. While it is more expensive than extract, there are recipes where it will really shine and elevate a dish. When it will make a wonderful addition to a dish, it has been listed as an ingredient, but it can always be replaced with vanilla extract in a one-to-one ratio.

WHITE CHOCOLATE

Made from cocoa butter, sugar, and milk, white chocolate contains no cocoa solids. It is much sweeter than dark chocolate and works well in baking to add a lovely, creamy sweetness.

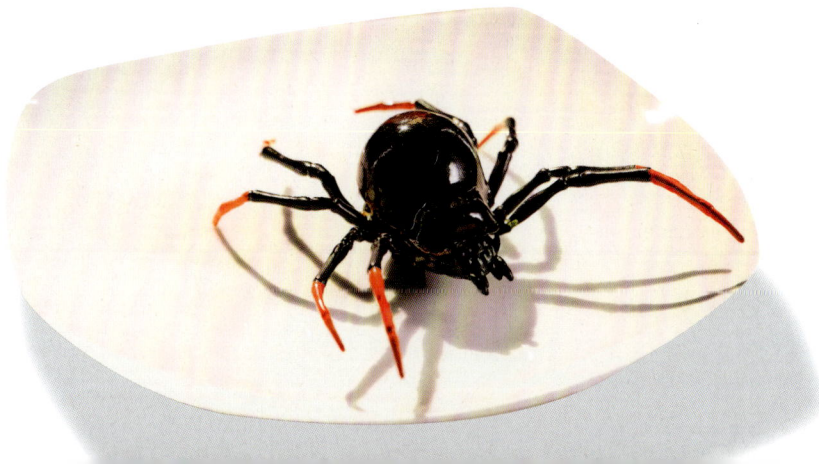

PLATFORM
9¾

ALL ABOARD!

The journey to Hogwarts— and baking glory—begins.

Shortly after discovering that he is a wizard in the *Harry Potter and the Sorcerer's Stone* movie, Harry finds himself at London's King's Cross station, navigating his journey to Hogwarts from Platform 9¾. As the place where Harry makes this important first step into his magical new life, this particular movie set made for a highly appropriate location for the opening task undertaken by the *Wizards of Baking* competing teams.

Few film worlds have captured our hearts and imaginations as completely as the Harry Potter movies. From *Harry Potter and the Sorcerer's Stone* to *Harry Potter and the Deathly Hallows—Parts 1 and 2*, each movie takes us on a journey of adventure, curiosity, inspiration, and celebration. Like Harry, the *Wizards of Baking* teams would find themselves visiting iconic locations, taking part in an epic competition that celebrates some of the finest sets from across the eight movies of the Harry Potter film series. Their first task required them to create a showpiece to reflect their joint Harry Potter connection, as well as showcase their individual baking specialties—and present it at Platform 9¾.

The movie scene that introduced the magical gateway was filmed at King's Cross on a Sunday afternoon. The station is renowned for its Victorian architecture, sporting two 800-foot-long train sheds topped by barrel-vaulted roofs, which is what the filmmakers wanted to showcase in the scene. Production designer Stuart Craig recalls: "We chose a platform that had big brick piers under big supporting arches that connected to another platform, which gave it a substantial wall to run at before they pass through it to the other side." As a result, the secret passageway to Platform 9¾ seen in the film is, in reality, situated between Platforms 4 and 5.

✳ Hemu and Riccardo

Riccardo's elementary school in Florence, Italy, had a willow tree and swing in the courtyard. Hemu has longed for a flying car ever since watching *Harry Potter and the Chamber of Secrets*. So, it is little surprise they chose to recreate the scene where Ron and Harry crash Arthur Weasley's flying car in the grounds of Hogwarts. The tree trunk is made with modeling chocolate and the car is almond cake with isomalt and fondant details. The chocolate spider bonbons contain caramel and peanut butter ganache that oozes out when bitten into.

Elizabeth and Juan

Elizabeth and Juan themed their bake around their favorite spell, the Patronus Charm, because it represents perseverance. The freestanding horse head, which is their Patronus Charm, is surrounded by chocolate swirls, as if it is currently being cast. Inspired by Butterbeer, it features cream mousse, Butterbeer caramel, and beer crémeux. The flavors are echoed by roasted malt mousse and almond praline in the base's rotating lily pads.

Zoë and Jordan

Zoë and Jordan's showpiece reflects the fact that they are both Hufflepuffs. A cake badger wearing a house scarf sits on top of a chocolate wall centerpiece that mimics the entrance to Platform 9¾. This represents the start of Harry's journey and the beginning of the bakers' own in the competition. Waving chocolate wands sends forth flying wafer paper Hogwarts acceptance letters! The suitcase cake is inspired by apple crumble and custard—an homage to classic English school lunches, referencing Zoë's roots.

Ashley and Kimberly

One of Ashley and Kimberly's favorite scenes is Harry's first Potions class. Their chocolate cabinet houses sugar bottles of ingredients used for potions such as Polyjuice Potion and Felix Felicis, also known as "Liquid Luck." Bubbling cauldrons and Tom Riddle's diary are made from cake. The lemon cake potion bottle, which includes lemon curd and elderflower buttercream, is a nod to Kimberly's husband, who loves lemon.

Jess and Jamie

Family-orientated Jess and Jamie's dessert replicates the Weasleys' home, The Burrow. Built from painted wafer paper, it is hidden inside a suitcase made of cake and chocolate. It sits on a cinnamon roll cake base, which Jamie makes for her relatives every Christmas. The rocks are deconstructed sweet potato pie—a dish that reminds Jess of family holidays.

✳ Miko and Chris

Proud Slytherins Miko and Chris are keen to highlight their house's more positive traits. Their fountain, made from cake, represents purity. A snake, shaped using rice cereal, symbolizes adaptability. Two tasting elements highlight the chefs' love for their cultures. Miko's Filipino heritage is referenced in the Earl Grey cake with calamansi curd. Chris's coconut passion fruit desserts, disguised as rocks, celebrate his Portuguese culture.

Conner and Michael

This isomalt recreation of the Mirror of Erised depicts the scene when Harry sees himself with his parents in the reflection. Conner and Michael are close to their mothers, and this design recalls the love shared by Harry and Lily. The stairs are a rose-scented cake with rose lychee gel—favorite flavors of Michael's mom. A vanilla bonbon symbolizes Conner's relationship with his mom, which he describes as "simple and pure."

Lisa and Mitzi

Spectrespecs ... a Quibbler ... it can only be Luna Lovegood's luggage! Luna is the favorite character of both Lisa and Mitzi, and her suitcase is a gluten-free Mexican chocolate cake with Abuelita chocolate cream. When worn, the Spectrespecs, made from white and raspberry chocolate with pop rocks, reveal the hidden message on the suitcase, "You're just as sane as I am."

Kayla and Yohann

Kayla and Yohann's showpiece is a celebration of *Harry Potter and the Sorcerer's Stone*. Balanced on Harry's wand, the first tier is a s'mores cake that looks like stone from Hogwarts Castle. Hagrid's infamous birthday cake for Harry sits on top, as do school acceptance letters. A Golden Snitch completes the design; it is popcorn mousse with caramel corn encased inside a chocolate shell.

TALENTED TEAMS

The nine skilled *Wizards of Baking* teams soon set about turning their creative visions into reality. The chefs' feelings of excitement, nervousness, and expectation would no doubt have been shared by Harry Potter when he set off from King's Cross for his first term at Hogwarts School of Witchcraft and Wizardry. For their first task, the teams were not competing against each other. Instead, they were trying to impress the judges—and earn a ticket to board the Hogwarts Express, their transport to the next round.

Jess and Jamie (above far left and left) named their design, "It's not much, but it's home," which are the words that Ron uses to introduce Harry to The Burrow in the *Harry Potter and the Chamber of Secrets* film. The chefs' showpiece included a tiny monitor in the kitchen, playing scenes from that movie. Dry ice added a mysterious fog effect, and small lights placed inside the suitcase highlighted key elements.

For their design, Conner (above center) and Michael were inspired by the love Lily and Harry have for each other. Their chocolate-framed Mirror of Erised lit up to reveal the mother and son hand-in-hand. Kayla and Yohann built and balanced a delicious creation that appeared to defy gravity (below right). It celebrated the *Harry Potter and the Sorcerer's Stone* movie, which Yohann saw with his dad, and a big bucket of popcorn, while Kayla watched it at her family's lake house, eating s'mores around a campfire.

Yet, despite the impressive designs and flavors of their showpieces, all three teams failed to gain a coveted ticket for the Hogwarts Express, cutting the competing field by a third. Although the judges made many complimentary comments, the desserts just fell short of the exacting standards required to succeed in *Wizards of Baking*.

SIX OF THE BEST

Hemu and Riccardo depicted their favorite scene of the Weasleys' flying car crashing into the Whomping Willow. At the tree's base sat spider bonbons, some of which scurried around, much to the consternation of the judges! Elizabeth and Juan took on the idea of perseverance in the form of a horse Patronus. Elizabeth connects with the theme of resilience in the films. For Juan, the movies mirrored his own journey, creating a "chosen" family through friendships. The Patronus Charm resonates with them both, underscoring the power of light in adversity.

Ashley and Kimberly took their inspiration from Professor Snape's Potions class, reminding Ashley of her childhood when she and her brother would create magical mixtures in their backyard! Cauldrons and bottles filled the chefs' showpiece, which also contained Gillyweed made from pistachio cake, mascarpone crema, and caramelized chocolate. Miko and Chris's design highlighted the lesser-known qualities of Slytherins. It had a troubled start, however, when Miko realized his cake hadn't cooked because the oven hadn't been turned on!

Lisa and Mitzi's trolley cart also had initial problems when their first cake burned and had to be started again from scratch. The chefs incorporated flavors, such as cajeta pastry cream, to highlight their shared pride in their Mexican heritage. Mitzi's specialty is molecular gastronomy, which she demonstrated by using a dehydrating technique to fashion the lenses of Luna's Spectrespecs. Zoë and Jordan's Hufflepuff celebration showpiece (page 26) also contained a station theme and included the entrance to Platform 9¾ below a cake badger, incorporating a mechanism that fired out Hogwarts acceptance letters.

It wasn't possible to pass through Zoë and Jordan's chocolate wall, even if doing it "at a run," if you were nervous! In the movies, the Hogwarts students did have the help of digital effects. However, for Harry's first attempt to reach the platform, a prop brick wall was built—it had a removable section, allowing actor Daniel Radcliffe access from one side to the other.

Aptly, the final scene of the eight films is also set on Platform 9¾, as Harry comforts his nervous son Albus, who is setting off for his first term. At the same place where he started his journey to Hogwarts as a young orphan, Harry has now taken on the role of protective parent. But while his journey had come full circle, the next task for the bakers was about to begin.

For the Cakes

3 cups (360 g) all-purpose flour

⅓ cup (35 g) cornstarch

¾ teaspoon salt

¾ teaspoon baking soda

2 teaspoons baking powder

2½ teaspoons ground cinnamon

1½ teaspoons ground nutmeg

1 teaspoon ground allspice

2 cups (400 g) brown sugar, packed

4 eggs

1⅓ cups (320 ml) unsweetened applesauce, homemade or store-bought

1⅓ cups (270 ml) canola oil

⅔ cup (165 ml) full-fat Greek yogurt, at room temperature

For the Apple Compote

3 Pink Lady (or similar) apples, peeled and finely chopped

½ teaspoon lemon zest, plus 2 teaspoons lemon juice

⅓ cup (70 g) brown sugar or more to taste

1 teaspoon ground cinnamon

½ teaspoon ground allspice

¼ teaspoon ground clove

Pinch of salt

2 teaspoons cornstarch mixed with 2 teaspoons water

For the Vanilla Custard Buttercream

2 cups (480 ml) whole milk

1 vanilla bean, split, with seeds scraped

⅔ cup (160 g) superfine cane sugar

¼ cup (30 g) cornstarch

3 large egg yolks

2 cups (450 g) unsalted butter, softened

For the Oat and Hazelnut Crumble

1 cup (120 g) all-purpose flour

1⅓ cups (120 g) old-fashioned rolled oats

1 cup (180 g) brown sugar

1 cup (120 g) toasted hazelnuts, coarsely chopped

½ teaspoon salt

9 tablespoons (120 g) unsalted butter, very soft

Prep time: 1 hour, plus cooling and chilling time

Cook time: 30 minutes

Zoë's Apple Crumble and Custard Cake

From *Wizards of Baking*, Episode 1: Platform 9¾

Zoë's spice cake was a hit with the judges—and now you can enjoy it, too, with her own recipe. Containing layers of zingy apple compote and vanilla custard buttercream, with the crunchy texture of hazelnut and oat crumble, it's a treat for your taste buds. The compote, buttercream, and crumble can all be made in advance.

TO MAKE THE CAKES

1. Preheat the oven to 350°F (180°C). Prepare three 8-inch round cake pans by greasing the base and sides and lining with parchment paper.

2. In a large bowl, whisk together the flour, cornstarch, salt, baking soda, baking powder, ground spices, and brown sugar. In a separate bowl, combine the eggs, applesauce, oil, and Greek yogurt. Fold the wet ingredients into the dry ingredients. Be careful not to overmix or bubbles will form in the cake. Divide the batter evenly among the prepared cake pans.

3. Bake for 25 to 30 minutes, checking after 25 minutes. The cakes are ready when an inserted skewer comes out clean. Leave to cool.

TO MAKE THE COMPOTE

1. In a large bowl, combine the apples, lemon zest and juice, brown sugar, ground spices, and salt, and leave to sit for 30 minutes.

2. Add the apple mixture to a pan and cook over medium-low heat for about 5 minutes. You want the apples to still have some bite to them! Increase the heat, then add the cornstarch slurry, and cook, stirring, until the apple juice bubbles. Remove from the heat.

TO MAKE THE CUSTARD BUTTERCREAM

1. In a pan, heat 1¾ cups (420 ml) of the milk with the vanilla seeds. Leave to infuse the flavor. In a bowl, whisk the superfine sugar, cornstarch, egg yolks, and remaining ¼ cup (60 ml) of milk into a paste and place in a pan over medium heat. Slowly pour over the vanilla-infused milk, whisking all the time until the custard thickens. Place in a bowl and cover with plastic wrap to prevent a skin from forming. Allow to cool.

2. In a bowl with a mixer, cream the butter until light and fluffy and then add the cooled custard one scoop at a time, beating continually until fully combined.

TO MAKE THE CRUMBLE

1. Preheat the oven to 350°F (180°C). Place all the ingredients in a bowl and stir until well combined. Place on a baking sheet and bake for 15 to 20 minutes until cooked and crispy. Break up with your fingers and allow the crumble pieces to cool.

TO ASSEMBLE THE CAKE

1. Trim the tops of the cakes if required. Place the custard buttercream into a piping bag and cut the end off. Take one of the cake layers and pipe a rim of buttercream around the perimeter of the cake to create a "wall." Scoop apple compote onto the cake and up to the wall of buttercream. Then spread a layer of buttercream over the apples, so they are completely encased. Sprinkle the crumble liberally over the top. Repeat for the next layer. Decorate the top of the cake using up any leftover buttercream and sprinkling crumble to finish.

ORIGINAL SHOW RECIPE!

CAKE INSPIRATION!

Zoë recommends always cooking with European butter. It has a higher butterfat content, which is better for baking and tends to have a richer, creamier flavor compared with American butter. She also suggests making sure that dairy and eggs are at room temperature when baking. This helps prevent your batter from splitting.

Jordan's
Abuelita Spice
Chocolate Crémeux

This is the recipe used by Jordan for Task 1. You can use it for decoration or between the layers of a cake.

1 teaspoon powdered gelatin

1 tablespoon water

⅔ cup (160 ml) whole milk

⅔ cup (160 ml) heavy cream

4 egg yolks (65 g), at room temperature

5 ounces (150 g) 64% dark chocolate, grated

1 teaspoon ground cinnamon

1 teaspoon ground nutmeg

½ teaspoon cayenne pepper

Prep time: 15 minutes, plus cooling and chilling time

Cook time: 15 minutes

1. Bloom the gelatin in the water.

2. Combine the milk and cream in a small saucepan. Bring to a boil. Once the cream is boiling, carefully mix in the egg yolks (tempering them) until thickened.

3. In a bowl, pour the hot cream mixture over the grated chocolate and bloomed gelatin and mix with an immersion blender until smooth. Stir in the cinnamon, nutmeg, and cayenne.

4. Refrigerate the crémeux overnight and use when ready.

"Where shall I put you? Let's see. I know ... Hufflepuff!"

—The Sorting Hat,
Harry Potter and the Sorcerer's Stone film

Chocolate Shortbread Wands

Inspired by Zoë and Jordan, Episode 1: Platform 9¾

For the Shortbread Wands

1 cup (225 g) unsalted butter, softened

½ cup (115 g) superfine sugar

2 teaspoons vanilla extract

3 tablespoons cornstarch

½ cup (50 g) cocoa powder

2 cups (250 g) all-purpose flour

Pinch of salt

For the Chocolate Crémeux

1 large egg

2 tablespoons superfine sugar

½ cup (120 ml) heavy cream

½ cup (120 ml) whole milk

3½ ounces (100 g) dark chocolate, chopped

For the Salted Caramel

5½ ounces (155 g) store-bought caramel

½ teaspoon kosher salt

2 ounces (55 g) cacao nibs

Prep time: 45 minutes,
plus cooling and chilling time

Cook time: 25 minutes

Jordan's wands, as pictured at right, involved Abuelita-spiced chocolate mousse, cocoa nib crunch, and salted caramel. This simplified version packs no less of a sweet hit for those craving a tasty wand but is simpler to make in crunchy chocolate shortbread, served with chocolate crémeux, salted caramel, and cacao nibs for a bit of extra crunch.

TO MAKE THE SHORTBREAD WANDS

1. Add the butter and superfine sugar to a food processor and whiz until smooth and well combined. Add the remaining ingredients and pulse until the mixture comes together, then transfer to a bowl and lightly knead until you have a smooth dough.

2. Line two large baking sheets with parchment paper. Divide the dough into roughly 2½-ounce (70-g) balls, then lay these on the baking sheets and shape into roughly 12-inch-long wand shapes, with one pointed end and one rounded end for the handle. You will have about 10 shortbread wands.

3. Transfer to the fridge and chill until firm, about 45 minutes.

4. Preheat the oven to 350°F (180°C). Bake the shortbreads for 15 minutes, then carefully remove from the oven. While still soft, use a palette knife to reshape them slightly, as they will have started to spread and lose their shape. Return to the oven for a further 10 minutes, until they feel firm and dry to the touch. Leave to cool completely on the baking sheets.

TO MAKE THE CHOCOLATE CRÉMEUX

1. Add the egg and superfine sugar to a mixing bowl and use a balloon whisk to mix together well. Heat the cream and milk in a small saucepan until just steaming, then pour over the egg mixture and whisk. Return this mixture to the saucepan and gently cook, stirring constantly, over low heat until the mixture has thickened slightly and is coating the back of the spoon. Add the chocolate to a heatproof bowl and pour the custard over it, gently stirring it until melted. Leave to cool for a few minutes, then chill until firm but still spreadable (45 minutes to 1 hour).

TO MAKE THE SALTED CARAMEL AND ASSEMBLE

1. Combine the caramel and salt in a small bowl, sprinkling a little extra salt on top if you like. Stir the crémeux to make it more spreadable, then spread or dip the crémeux over the handle part of the chocolate shortbreads and lay these out on a serving plate. Scatter the cacao nibs over the crémeux, lightly pressing them in so that they stick slightly, and serve with the caramel and any extra crémeux on the side to dip the shortbread wands in.

> "It seems only yesterday that your mother and father were in here buying their first wands."
>
> —Garrick Ollivander,
> *Harry Potter and the Sorcerer's Stone* film

CAKE INSPIRATION!

Jordan's super-neat wands were made using rolled sheets of plastic. Our "inspired by" recipe, left, produces a slightly less pin-neat result, but matches the flavor and crunch of the original.

Dear Judges,

We are pleased to inform you that you have been accepted to come on an edible, enchanted journey with Zoe and Jordan.

As judges, you will be required to put your expertise and creative imagination to

THE JUDGES
Platform 9 ¾
Warner Bros. Studios,
Leavesden

Elderflower Potion Bottle Cake

Inspired by Ashley and Kimberly, Episode 1: Platform 9¾

✳

For the Cakes

10½ ounces (300 g) unsalted butter, softened

1½ cups (340 g) superfine sugar

Zest and juice of 2 lemons

4 medium eggs, at room temperature

¼ cup (65 g) plain yogurt

2 cups (280 g) self-rising flour

3 tablespoons elderflower cordial

For the Elderflower Swiss Meringue Buttercream

2 large egg whites, about 2½ ounces (70 g)

5 ounces (140 g) superfine sugar

7 ounces (200 g) unsalted butter, softened

2 tablespoons elderflower cordial

For the Chocolate Frosting

3½ ounces (100 g) dark chocolate, chopped

7 ounces (200 g) unsalted butter, softened

2½ cups (300 g) powdered sugar

1 to 2 tablespoons milk

For the Cake Layers

2 ounces (55 g) store-bought lemon curd

Prep time: 1 hour, plus cooling and chilling time

Cook time: 40 minutes

> "I can teach you how to bewitch the mind and ensnare the senses. I can tell you how to bottle fame, brew glory, and even put a stopper in death."
>
> —Professor Severus Snape, *Harry Potter and the Sorcerer's Stone* film

Professor Snape's introduction to Potions class in *Harry Potter and the Sorcerer's Stone* remains one of Kimberly and Ashley's all-time favorite scenes. Their potion bottle—the first tasting element in their showpiece design—combined the flavors of lemon and elderflower, as does this recipe, adapted to have a simpler buttercream-finish exterior.

TO MAKE THE CAKES

1. Preheat the oven to 350°F (180°C). Prepare two 9-inch springform cake pans by greasing the base and sides and lining with parchment paper.

2. In a large mixing bowl, add the butter, superfine sugar, and lemon zest and beat using a handheld electric mixer until pale and fluffy (3 to 4 minutes). Alternatively, you can do this in a stand mixer. Add the eggs one at a time, beating well between each addition, then whisk in the yogurt. Gently fold the flour through until combined.

3. Divide the batter between the prepared cake pans and bake for 35 to 40 minutes, until risen, golden brown, and a skewer inserted into the center comes out clean.

4. Meanwhile, stir together the lemon juice and elderflower cordial in a cup with a spout. When the cakes are cooked and out of the oven, use a skewer to prick holes all over them. Pour over the lemon mixture, then leave to cool in the pans.

TO MAKE THE BUTTERCREAM

1. Add the egg whites and superfine sugar to a heatproof mixing bowl, or the bowl of a stand mixer, and whisk together. Place over a pan of barely simmering water, making sure the base of the bowl doesn't touch the water, then continue to whisk until the sugar has dissolved. You can test this by touching the mixture with your fingers; when you can no longer feel any grains of sugar, it is ready (4 to 5 minutes).

2. Remove the bowl from the pan and use a handheld electric mixer or stand mixer with the whisk attachment to whisk the mixture until stiff peaks have formed (10 to 15 minutes). Gradually add the butter, a tablespoon at a time, until the mixture is really thick and glossy. If the mixture starts to look loose at any point, keep whisking to thicken. Add the elderflower cordial and whisk. Cover and set aside.

TO MAKE THE FROSTING

1. Melt the chocolate in a heatproof bowl set over a pan of barely simmering water, then set aside to cool.

2. Add the butter and powdered sugar to a mixing bowl and mix together using a handheld electric mixer until pale and fluffy (3 to 4 minutes). Alternatively, you can do this in a stand mixer. Whisk in the chocolate and milk until it has a smooth and spreadable consistency, then set aside.

TO ASSEMBLE YOUR CAKE

1. Using pastry cutters, cut out three 4-inch circles, one 3-inch circle, and one 2-inch circle from the cakes. Lay one of the 4-inch circles on a cake board, then place this on a cake-decorating turntable. Spread some of the elderflower buttercream on top of this, then add a little of the lemon curd and spread evenly. Continue to stack the remaining 4-inch circles, then the 3-inch circle, then the 2-inch circle, spreading the buttercream and lemon curd between each layer.

2. Transfer the chocolate frosting to a piping bag, then pipe the frosting around the cake. Use an angled palette knife to spread the frosting very thinly around the edges of the cake, creating a bottle shape. This first layer of buttercream is the "crumb coat," so don't worry too much about making it really neat at this stage. Chill the cake until firm (45 minutes to 1 hour).

3. Once the cake is firm, continue to pipe the frosting around the edges, using the palette knife to firm up the bottle shape. Pipe a little more on top to create the look of a bottle top, using the palette knife to smooth any edges.

4. This cake can be chilled for up to 2 days before serving.

Jam Pastry Acceptance Letters

Inspired by *Wizards of Baking*, Episode 1: Platform 9¾

For the Seals

12 red candy melts

Ice water

1 to 2 tablespoons unsalted butter, softened

For the Pastry

2½ cups (310 g) all-purpose flour

½ cup (60 g) powdered sugar

1 teaspoon kosher salt

¾ cup (170 g) unsalted butter, very cold

¼ cup (55 g) vegetable shortening, very cold

6 tablespoons (90 ml) ice water

1 cup (325 g) jam, in the flavor of your choice

1 egg, lightly beaten with 1 tablespoon water, for egg wash

Special Equipment

2 or more Hogwarts wax stamps

Prep time: 2 hours, plus cooling and chilling time

Cook time: 30 minutes

The Hogwarts acceptance letter is one of the most iconic props from the first film and possibly the whole movie series. It has been reimagined here in the sweetest form yet, as a delicious pastry bursting with a jam of your choice! The famous letter was also featured in the showpieces created by Kayla and Yohann, and Zoë and Jordan, for this task.

TO MAKE THE SEALS

1. Preheat the oven to 200°F (95°C). Space out 8 candy melts on a parchment-lined cookie sheet. Reserve the remaining candy melts. Fill a bowl with ice water, and place the wax stamps inside it. Have a paper towel and the butter close by.

2. Place the cookie sheet with the candy melts in the oven for 1½ to 2 minutes, until the melts are shiny and beginning to melt but are still holding their shape. Remove the sheet from the oven and slip the parchment onto a second, cool, cookie sheet. Allow the melts to rest for 2 to 3 minutes so they set a bit. Turn off the oven.

3. Pull a stamp from the ice water. Grease the paper towel with a bit of butter, and wipe down the stamp, removing any water, and greasing slightly. Press the seal into the center of a candy melt, and allow it to sit undisturbed for 45 to 90 seconds. Twist off from the candy melt. Place the stamp back in the ice water for about 30 seconds, or if using multiple stamps, select a fresh one to do the next seal. Seals that do not turn out as desired can be returned to the oven and remelted.

TO MAKE THE PASTRY

1. In a large bowl, combine the flour, powdered sugar, and salt. Use a pastry cutter to cut the butter and shortening into the flour mixture until it resembles a coarse crumb. Pour about half of the ice water over the flour-butter mixture, and use the pastry cutter to blend until a shaggy dough comes together. Add a bit more water as needed to bring all the flour into the dough. Split the dough in half, wrap both halves in parchment paper, and allow to rest in the refrigerator for 30 minutes.

2. Roll out a disk of dough to a 9-by-14-inch rectangle. Trim to square it up, reserving the scraps. With a sharp knife, cut the dough into 8 "envelope" pieces about 3 by 4½ inches. Repeat with the second disk of dough. Refrigerate all the pieces for 15 minutes.

3. Roll out the scraps, and use them to cut 8 triangle-shaped pieces, with a long side of about 4 inches. Working with pairs of rectangular pieces, brush the edges with egg wash and sandwich 2 tablespoons of jam in the center of each pair. Crimp the edges all the way around with a fork and place a triangle on top against one of the long edges, to create the flap. Crimp along the joined edge with the fork to seal. Brush the triangle with egg wash. Using a paring knife, cut a small slit under the point of the triangle. Once assembled, refrigerate for another 15 minutes.

4. Preheat the oven to 400°F (200°C). Bake the pastry for 20 to 25 minutes, until golden brown and crisp. When the pastries are cool, melt any leftover candy melts and use to attach the seals.

> "We are pleased to inform you that you have been accepted at Hogwarts School of Witchcraft and Wizardry."
>
> —Harry Potter,
> reading his acceptance letter,
> *Harry Potter and the Sorcerer's Stone* film

Hagrid's "Happee Birthdae" Cupcakes

Inspired by *Wizards of Baking*, Episode 1: Platform 9¾

For the Cupcakes

1½ cups (180 g) cake flour

1 cup (100 g) unsweetened cocoa powder

1 teaspoon baking powder

1 teaspoon baking soda

½ teaspoon salt

½ cup (120 ml) milk, at room temperature

½ cup (120 g) sour cream

4 large eggs, at room temperature

1 cup (200 g) granulated sugar

1 cup (200 g) light brown sugar, packed

½ cup plus 1 tablespoon (135 ml) vegetable oil

1 tablespoon vanilla extract

For the Frosting

1 cup (225 g) unsalted butter, softened

8 cups (960 g) powdered sugar

½ cup (120 ml) half-and-half

1 tablespoon vanilla extract

Pinch of salt

3 or 4 drops pink food coloring

2 drops green food coloring

Prep time: 45 minutes, plus cooling time

Cook time: 20 minutes

Hagrid was the unlikely baker of Harry's first ever birthday cake, as seen in *Harry Potter and the Sorcerer's Stone*. In *Wizards of Baking*, a version also sat atop Kayla and Yohann's showpiece in Episode 1. Here, we've reimagined the design as a tray of delicious chocolate cupcakes.

TO MAKE THE CUPCAKES

1. Preheat the oven to 350°F (180°C). Place cupcake liners in two muffin pans. Set aside.

2. In a large bowl, whisk together the flour, cocoa powder, baking powder, baking soda, and salt until combined. Set aside.

3. Combine the milk and sour cream in a small measuring bowl or jar and set aside.

4. In a separate medium bowl, whisk the eggs, granulated sugar, brown sugar, oil, and vanilla until combined. Pour approximately half the egg mixture into the dry ingredients. Add half the milk and sour cream mixture, and gently combine. Add to combine the remaining mixtures, until a thin batter forms. Pour the batter into the prepared cupcake liners, filling each one halfway.

5. Bake for 18 to 20 minutes, or until a toothpick comes out clean. Remove the cupcakes to a wire rack, and allow to cool completely before frosting.

TO MAKE THE FROSTING

1. While the cupcakes are cooling, use a hand mixer on medium speed to cream the butter, powdered sugar, half-and-half, vanilla, and salt in a mixing bowl, scraping down the sides as necessary, until light and fluffy.

2. Remove 1 cup (125 g) of frosting to a separate small bowl.

3. Add drops of pink food coloring to your main frosting bowl and continue mixing until you've achieved your desired color. Depending on the temperature in your kitchen, this may take a few minutes, so stick with it.

4. Mix the 1 cup (125 g) of reserved white icing with the green food coloring, and place in a piping bag. Set aside.

5. Once the icing is nice and fluffy, ice the cooled cupcakes with the pink frosting. It's okay if it's a little sloppy—this is Hagrid's work you're replicating!

6. Once all the cupcakes are frosted, pipe the letters in green icing onto the top of your cupcakes. Do one letter per cupcake to spell the message "Happee Birthdae," and decorate the rest with lightning bolts or other Harry Potter symbols.

"Afraid I might have sat on it at some point, but I imagine it'll taste fine just the same."

—Rubeus Hagrid, *Harry Potter and the Sorcerer's Stone* film

GRINGOTTS

BANKING
ON SUCCESS

The chefs require good fortune
for their next challenge.

Gringotts Wizarding Bank is situated at an intersection in Diagon Alley. A place of contradictions, the asymmetrical columns on the building's exterior look like it is close to collapse. Inside, however, is a scene of opulence, with two long rows of smartly suited tellers. Underneath the marbled hall is a network of locked vaults, brimming with coins, jewels, and magical artifacts. Unsurprisingly, Gringotts provided a wealth of inspiration for the six *Wizards of Baking* teams, from its marbled entrance to the subterranean caves. Of course, any culinary error would prove very costly indeed.

Gringotts is first seen in the *Harry Potter and the Sorcerer's Stone* film. Escorted to Diagon Alley by Rubeus Hagrid, Harry worries that he won't be able to afford any of the school supplies he requires, as he doesn't have any money. Hagrid explains his funds can be found at Gringotts, and the pair are soon traveling underground to Vault 687, where Harry is astounded to see stacks of gold coins, bequeathed to him by his parents. A visit to Vault 713 follows, allowing Hagrid to retrieve the Sorcerer's Stone, so that it can be transported to Hogwarts.

Above ground, Gringotts has the old-world look of an austere banking organization. Production designer Stuart Craig explains: "Banks are traditionally symbols of stability. That is the intention in bank architecture—to convey a feeling of reassurance." For this scene, the filmmakers decided to use a real-life location, wanting somewhere spacious and ostentatious, contrasting with the smaller dimensions of the staff employed there. Australia House, which is the longest continuously occupied foreign mission in London, was selected. Its Beaux Arts interior provided the proportions that the film crew desired.

The bank's interior also features in *Harry Potter and the Deathly Hallows— Part 2*. For this film, the banking hall was built as a set at Leavesden Studios. It was here that the *Wizards of Baking* teams presented their Gringotts-themed creations. As if the pressure weren't already high enough, Warwick Davis, who played Gringotts' Griphook in the final two movies, joined the judging panel to sample the incredible edibles.

Elizabeth and Juan

Marbled chocolate columns against hand-painted fondant prove the perfect materials to replicate one of the bank's counters. A secret compartment opens to reveal a sleeping dragon wrapped around the Sorcerer's Stone, which are made from raspberry Champagne sponge with raspberry crémeux. Elizabeth's money bags also use Champagne sponge, with Chambord icing.

✳ Zoë and Jordan

Zoë and Jordan had a light bulb moment for their design—a glorious isomalt chandelier! Zoë's marble pillar is a dark whiskey-soaked chocolate cake with salted caramel whiskey buttercream. Jordan's mouthwatering Galleons rise up from the center of the floor on a platform. They combine strawberries with white chocolate, tarragon, and mint, as Gringotts is reminiscent of London's Royal Mint, where coins and medals are made.

Lisa and Mitzi

There are plenty of twists and turns with Lisa and Mitzi's intricate design—and it looks like the upturned cart perched at the top couldn't cope with them. Coins and gems spill out around the chocolate tracks toward the ominous sight of a dragon's tail at the bottom. An isomalt Thief's Downfall completes the defensive enchantments.

Miko and Chris

This sublime design features stalactites and stalagmites made from carved cake covered with fondant and topped with crispies covered in chocolate. The central showpiece sits on a spinning table so that it constantly moves. A train brings the tasting elements—gold coins made from beet gel, chocolate ganache, and crystallized thyme.

✳ Hemu and Riccardo

This is one Gringotts vault that even Harry, Ron, and Hermione might be unable to enter. The cake dragon guards treasures, including wizarding books, made from vanilla cake with strawberry buttercream. Riccardo's hidden jewels are made from raspberry blancmange on a shortbread biscuit.

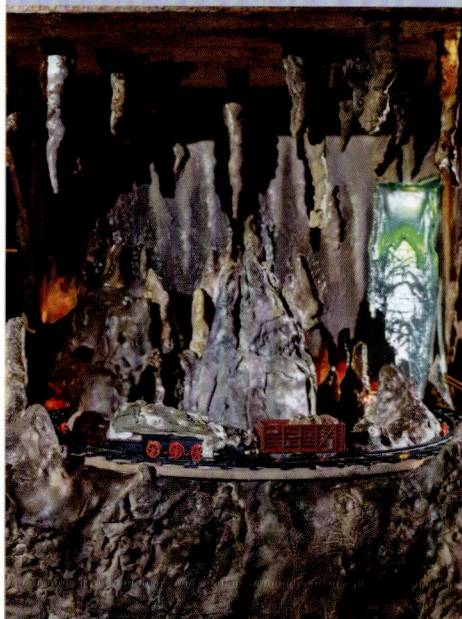

Ashley and Kimberly

From the bank exterior in Diagon Alley to the underground vaults, Kimberly and Ashley's bake shows both sides of Gringotts. The vaults do not give up their treasures easily—one must be opened with a key, while another has a chocolate door that melts away with hot caramel sauce. Inside can be found a chocolate replica of Godric Gryffindor's sword, the Sorcerer's Stone, and an array of colorful jewels spilling out across the floor.

BANKING AND BAKING

From marble columns and money bags to creepy caves and golden Galleons, the chefs' inventiveness came to the fore in the second *Wizards of Baking* challenge. Kimberly and Ashley (above far left) were the only team to adopt the ambitious approach of recreating Gringotts above and below ground. They wanted to include rare and rich flavors, since Gringotts is a repository for treasures and jewels. The outside of the cave was made from Madagascar vanilla bean cake, soaked with orange liqueur and topped with Italian buttercream. Chocolatier Ashley's gold nuggets also featured vanilla bean with saffron ganache.

The other teams honed in on details at the bank, such as Zoë and Jordan (above left), whose design focused on the cool marble and decadent chandeliers found in Gringotts's main hall. Whiskey was used in the cake, as the chefs imagined the bankers might sip on this refined drink after a hard day counting money. Jordan's strawberry, white chocolate, tarragon, and mint Galleons looked as tempting as the ones featured in the Gringotts scene in the first Harry Potter movie! Those metal props frequently disappeared while on location. When Gringotts featured again in *Harry Potter and the Deathly Hallows—Part 2*, the coins were made of plastic and glued together in stacks!

Hemu and Riccardo (above center) ventured underground for their treasure-filled vault guarded by a frightening dragon, which used light and smoke to create a fire-breathing effect. Edible skulls and jewels littered the floor for anyone hungry enough to risk approaching!

ROCKY RECIPES

Chris and Miko (above right) also took a subterranean approach. For their rock formation, they decided to use ingredients that grow under the soil, such as beets and ube, also known as purple yam. Ube is one of the most popular traditional Filipino dessert ingredients, allowing Miko to showcase his culture. He also included feuilletine, to add some crunch and texture, similar to soil or rocks.

Terrifying tracks twisted around Lisa and Mitzi's design (bottom center). Their rocky road cake base featured a whipped Chantilly cream with candied peanuts, marshmallow, chocolate-covered potato chips, and chocolate chips—as full of treasures as Gringotts itself! Mitzi is very fond of rocky road, as it was the first ice cream flavor she tried after moving from Mexico to the United States. Their design was completed with numerous hanging gems made from chocolate bonbons. The chefs probably wished they could use the *Gemino* curse for these! In *Harry Potter and the Deathly Hallows—Part 2*, the Lestranges' vault at Gringotts was protected by this spell, which created multiple versions of everything touched by an intruder.

While Ashley and Kimberly sadly left the contest at this stage, it was Elizabeth and Juan who were crowned winners of the second task, with their impressive bank counter and hidden dragon (page 46). Both chefs combined fruity flavors with Champagne, a drink that exudes opulence, in their tasting elements—money bag cakes and the Sorcerer's Stone. The judges agreed that the team's success was richly deserved.

Zoë's Chocolate Whiskey Cake

From *Wizards of Baking*, Episode 2: Gringotts

For the Cakes

5 ounces (140 g) 60 to 70% dark chocolate

2 tablespoons unsweetened cocoa

⅔ cup (160 ml) strong brewed black coffee, warm

⅓ cup (80 ml) whiskey or bourbon

1¾ cups (240 g) all-purpose flour

1 teaspoon baking soda

½ teaspoon salt

1 cup (225 g) unsalted butter, softened

1⅓ cups (300 g) superfine cane sugar

1 tablespoon vanilla bean paste

3 large eggs, at room temperature

For the Whiskey Salted Caramel

1 cup minus 2 tablespoons (200 g) superfine cane sugar

6 tablespoons (85 g) unsalted butter, cubed

½ cup (120 ml) heavy cream

1 teaspoon flaky salt (such as Maldon)

Whiskey to taste

For the Swiss Meringue Buttercream

5 egg whites (180 g)

1½ cups (360 g) superfine cane sugar

2 cups plus 3 tablespoons (540 g) unsalted butter, cubed

Prep time: 2 hours, plus cooling time

Cook time: 35 minutes

There are plenty of treasures securely hidden away at Gringotts. Thankfully, Zoë has decided not to keep this recipe for her delicious chocolate whiskey cake under lock and key! With a whiskey caramel buttercream, gold chocolate crunch, and rich ganache, this is an opulent dessert. The caramel, gold nuggets, and ganache can all be made ahead of time.

TO MAKE THE CAKES

1. Preheat the oven to 350°F (180°C). Prepare three 7-inch round cake pans by greasing the base and sides and lining with parchment paper.

2. Melt the chocolate using a bain-marie or in the microwave and allow to cool. In a cup with a spout, mix the cocoa with the warm coffee. Add the whiskey. In a bowl, combine the flour, baking soda, and salt.

3. In a stand mixer, cream the butter, superfine sugar, and vanilla until light and fluffy. Add the eggs one by one, scraping the bowl in between each addition. Add the cooled chocolate and beat for another minute. Next, add the dry ingredients and coffee mix, alternating between the dry and wet ingredients and finishing with the dry ingredients, then mix until the batter is well combined. Divide evenly among the prepared cake pans, place in the oven, and bake for 30 to 35 minutes, checking after 30 minutes. Remove from the oven and cool on wire racks.

TO MAKE THE CARAMEL

1. Heat the superfine sugar in a pan over medium heat until it melts and turns a deep amber color. Take off the heat and vigorously stir in the cubed butter piece by piece.

2. Once the butter has melted, slowly pour in the cream, stirring the whole time. Put back on the heat and cook for a further minute to bubble and thicken.

3. Remove from the heat and stir in the flaky salt and whiskey to taste. Pour into a sterilized jar and allow to cool before using. Note: If you don't have time, you can use store-bought salted caramel and fold in a little whiskey instead.

TO MAKE THE BUTTERCREAM

1. Weigh out the egg whites. Measure twice that weight of superfine sugar and three times that weight of butter (or directly follow the gram weights listed). Place the egg whites and sugar in the bowl of a stand mixer and place the bowl over a pan of simmering water. Stir until all the sugar has melted.

2. Place the bowl on the stand mixer, add the whisk attachment, and whisk until stiff peaks form and the bowl is no longer hot to the touch. Switch to the paddle attachment and slowly add the butter, one cube at a time, until it has all been combined and the buttercream is light and fluffy.

3. Fold in the whiskey salted caramel to taste.

For the Gold Crunch Nuggets

3½ ounces (100 g) milk chocolate

1 cup (30 g) toasted rice cereal

1 teaspoon vanilla bean paste

Edible gold luster dust

For the Ganache

1 pound (450 g) 60% dark chocolate, chopped

½ cup (120 ml) Baileys Irish Cream liqueur

½ cup (120 ml) heavy cream

TO MAKE THE GOLD CRUNCH NUGGETS

1. Melt the milk chocolate in a bowl over a bain-marie or in the microwave. Stir in the rice cereal and vanilla. Then, drop tiny spoonfuls of the mixture onto a baking sheet lined with parchment paper. Allow to set until firm. Once set, toss the nuggets in some gold luster dust until they are fully coated.

TO MAKE THE GANACHE

1. Melt the chopped chocolate in a bowl over a bain-marie. Remove from the heat. In a separate pan, gently heat the Baileys and cream until the liquid begins to simmer at the edges. Pour the cream over the chocolate. Leave for 3 minutes and then stir until smooth.

> ## "Gringotts, the wizard bank. Ain't no safer place, not one. Except perhaps Hogwarts."
>
> —Rubeus Hagrid,
> *Harry Potter and the Sorcerer's Stone* film

— ✦ —

TO ASSEMBLE THE CAKE

1. When the cakes are cool, spread the buttercream on one cake and sprinkle the crunchy gold nuggets on top, stacking the next cake layer and repeating. Reserve a few gold nuggets. Once stacked, cover the cake top and sides with the ganache and decorate the top of the cake with the remaining gold nuggets.

CAKE INSPIRATION!

Zoë recommends weighing out ingredients, as it is more accurate and will help ensure a successful bake.

Champagne and Raspberry Money Bag Cake

Inspired by Elizabeth and Juan, Episode 2: Gringotts

For the Cakes

5½ ounces (155 g) raspberries

13¼ ounces (375 g) unsalted butter, softened

13¼ ounces (375 g) superfine sugar

5 medium eggs

1 tablespoon vanilla extract

13¼ ounces (375 g) self-rising flour

¾ teaspoon baking powder

3 tablespoons Champagne or other sparkling wine

A few drops of pink food coloring

For the Raspberry and White Chocolate Swiss Meringue Buttercream

2 large egg whites, about 2½ ounces (70 g)

5 ounces (140 g) superfine sugar

7 ounces (200 g) unsalted butter, softened

2 ounces (55 g) white chocolate, chopped

2 tablespoons Chambord or other raspberry liqueur

For Decoration

35 ounces (990 g) fondant icing

¼ cup (30 g) cocoa powder

A handful of chocolate coins

Prep time: 1 hour 15 minutes, plus cooling time

Cook time: 45 minutes

"Mr. Harry Potter
wishes to make
a withdrawal."

—Rubeus Hagrid,
Harry Potter and the Sorcerer's Stone film

A money bag from Gringotts Bank inspired the clever replica component of Elizabeth and Juan's episode-winning showpiece design. Our homage recipe retains their flavor profiles of Champagne and raspberry, with decadent ingredients and a brightly colored cake cunningly concealed under fondant icing.

TO MAKE THE CAKES

1. Preheat the oven to 350°F (180°C). Prepare two 9-inch springform cake pans by greasing the base and sides and lining with parchment paper.

2. Add the raspberries to a small bowl and mash with a fork until fairly smooth. Set aside.

3. In a large mixing bowl, add the butter and superfine sugar and beat using a handheld electric mixer until pale and fluffy (3 to 4 minutes). Alternatively, you can do this in a stand mixer. Add the eggs one at a time, beating well between each addition, then add the vanilla and whisk. Gently fold the flour, baking powder, raspberries, Champagne, and food coloring through, until well combined and you have a batter of a pale pink color, adding a few more food coloring drops if needed.

4. Divide the batter between the prepared pans. Level the surface and bake for 40 to 45 minutes, until risen, golden brown, and a skewer inserted into the middle comes out clean. Transfer to a wire rack and leave to cool completely in the pans.

TO MAKE THE BUTTERCREAM

1. Place the egg whites and superfine sugar in a heatproof mixing bowl, or the bowl of a stand mixer, and use a balloon whisk to stir together. Place over a bowl of barely simmering water, making sure the base of the bowl doesn't touch the water, and continue to whisk until the sugar has dissolved. You can test this by touching the mixture with your fingers; when you can no longer feel any grains of sugar between your fingers, it is ready (4 to 5 minutes).

2. Remove the bowl from the pan and use a handheld electric mixer or stand mixer with the whisk attachment to beat the mixture until stiff peaks have formed (10 to 15 minutes). Now, gradually add the butter, a tablespoon at a time, until the mixture is really thick and glossy. If the mixture starts to look loose at any point, just keep whisking until it has thickened.

3. Melt the white chocolate in a heatproof bowl set over a pan of barely simmering water, making sure the base doesn't touch the water. Stir until melted, then set aside to cool for a few minutes. Add the white chocolate and Chambord to the buttercream, whisking until it has thickened. Cover and set aside until needed.

3. On a work surface, lay out the fondant icing. Sprinkle over the cocoa powder, kneading the icing until it is smooth and pliable and has become evenly brown all over with no pockets of cocoa powder remaining. Roll the icing out to a roughly 12-by-12-inch circle. Then, carefully use the rolling pin to lay this on top of the cake, making sure to get the center of the icing over the tip of the cake. Use your hands to smooth down the sides as much as possible. Don't worry if there are a few creases where the icing has overlapped. Use a sharp knife to trim the excess icing from around the base of the cake.

4. Take a small ball of the remaining icing and roll out to a roughly 4-inch circle. Pinch this together at the center to create a top for your money bag. Gently press this into the top of the cake. Take another small piece of icing and roll it out to a long, thin strip and use this to go around the base of the top of the money bag, leaving two pieces hanging down to look like string. Serve with chocolate coins.

TO DECORATE

1. To assemble the cakes, use a large serrated knife to level each of the tops to make them flat. Cut out two 4-inch circles with a pastry cutter, then cut one 3½-inch circle, followed by one 2½-inch circle. Use a serrated knife to trim the top of the smallest circle so that it has a slightly pointed top. Transfer some of the buttercream to a piping bag.

2. Lay one of the 4-inch circles on a cake board. Place this on a cake-decorating turntable. Pipe some of the buttercream over the top and use an angled palette knife to smooth it. Top with the other 4-inch circle, and repeat using buttercream between the layers, adding the 3½-inch circle and finishing with the smallest pointed circle on top. Pipe the remaining buttercream around the edges of the cake and use the palette knife to smooth the sides.

DIAGON
ALLEY

TREATS
IN STORES

Will the bakers' showpieces
be top of the shops?

The *Wizards of Baking* teams' recipes feature some unusual ingredients to elevate their amazing creations. The shopping lists for this task included passion fruit purée, feuilletine, gold Callebaut chocolate, and rose petals. These aren't the items you'd find in your local grocery store, but there are specialty shops that can satisfy every chef's requirements. In the *Harry Potter and the Sorcerer's Stone* film, the eleven-year-old wizard was faced with a similar dilemma, needing to buy some unusual objects for his first term at Hogwarts. Thankfully for him, Rubeus Hagrid knows the right place to go, escorting him to the wonderful Diagon Alley.

At this shopping district for wizards and witches, owls and bats look down on Harry from their perches, as a gaggle of excitable children stare through a window at the new Nimbus 2000. Flea markets and junk shops were raided for weeks by the filmmakers to ensure that the Dickensian-looking buildings were well stocked. The purchases had to be made in secret, however, as no details about the first Harry Potter film could be revealed. One assistant, who bought brooms in bulk, simply told the retailer that she had a lot of sweeping to do!

One of the most memorable moments is Harry's visit to Ollivanders, which is replicated in dessert form by Hemu and Riccardo. Around 17,000 wand boxes were created for the movie set, each hand-stamped with the Ollivanders logo. The shop forms part of the Diagon Alley set at the Warner Bros. Harry Potter Studio Tour at Leavesden, Hertfordshire, UK, which is where the bakers presented their desserts for this task. As an additional challenge, the teams had to market their wares to an invited audience of Harry Potter film fans.

In *Harry Potter and the Half-Blood Prince*, half of the shops in the alley have closed down, but one new store is thriving—Weasleys' Wizard Wheezes. All the Diagon Alley shops had previously conformed to a subdued color palette for their design. For the Weasley twins' new business, that theme was broken to give it a brash, bright look. Lisa and Mitzi celebrated Fred and George's successful enterprise with their joke shop treats—one of five clever *Wizards of Baking* Diagon Alley–inspired designs.

Zoë and Jordan

Flourish and Blotts provides inspiration for Zoë and Jordan's showpiece—mini books that are worth getting your teeth into. Olive oil, rosemary, and thyme cakes are adorned with raspberry jelly and lemon mousse. The flavors are directly inspired by rosewood, lemonwood, and olivewood, evoking the shop's fixtures, books, and paper.

✳ Elizabeth and Juan

Destined to become the youngest Hogwarts Quidditch player in a century, Harry is fascinated by one particular shop in Diagon Alley. Elizabeth and Juan commemorate Quality Quidditch Supplies with their pitch flanked by towers for spectators. Of course, every Quidditch pitch needs a Golden Snitch. These are made from peanut mousse, peanut cake, pretzel chocolate crunch, nougat, and praline. This winning combination is encased in a thin chocolate shell with delicate, flexible wings.

Miko and Chris

Every Hogwarts first year student must be equipped with a standard size 2 pewter cauldron, so a visit to Potage's Cauldron Shop is essential. Miko and Chris's dessert logs and bubbles both feature layers of crème fraîche cake, cider gelée, apple butter, smoked caramel mousse, and rosemary white chocolate crunch.

Lisa and Mitzi

Their showpiece's raised top hat can only mean that Lisa and Mitzi are taking a trip to Weasleys' Wizard Wheezes. The chefs create two classic Weasley products— screaming yo-yos and chattering teeth. These sit on a conveyor belt, with new treats continually appearing underneath the hat.

Hemu and Riccardo

Ollivanders is packed from floor to ceiling with boxes, but inside Hemu and Riccardo's version, you'll find raspberry and coconut rather than wands. Each box has layers of dark chocolate, raspberry mousse, raspberry gelée, coconut dacquoise, and vanilla raspberry mousseline sponge, all encased in a chocolate shell. A tempting coconut semifreddo wand encased in a thin layer of milk chocolate sits on top.

TALKING SHOPS

Task 3 saw the teams inspired by different shops in Diagon Alley. Miko and Chris (above far left) used apple and caramel flavors for their bubbling cauldron. Chris grew up in Boston and used to go apple-picking in the nearby orchards. Miko loves caramel, as it reminds him of yema, a Filipino dessert similar to dulce de leche. Lisa and Mitzi (above far right) have always wanted to drink pumpkin juice at Hogwarts, so they incorporated the fruit into their joke shop bakes. Their tasting elements featured golden chocolate crémeux, passion fruit jam, fresh passion fruit seeds, pumpkin iota filling, and feuilletine cookie batter all covered in chocolate couverture.

Zoë and Jordan's mini books (bottom right) featured the old-fashioned aroma of rose and the healing properties of herbs, paired with zesty lemon. The raspberry gelée and mousse in Hemu and Riccardo's wand boxes (above center and bottom left) rekindled happy memories for the Italian-born chef. Riccardo said: "When I was a kid, I used to spend part of the summer at our house in the Alps. My family used to go for walks around a nearby lake called Barcis, and we would pick raspberries and eat them as we were walking on the lake shore." Unfortunately, Diagon Alley proved to be the end of the road for these two chefs.

Elizabeth and Juan's dessert (above right and page 58), inspired by Quality Quidditch Supplies, used peanut and pretzel flavors, as they are the chefs' favorite snacks to eat at sporting events. Fittingly, given the competitive theme, they were judged the winning team of this round.

Olive Oil, Rosemary, Lemon, and Thyme Book Cakes

Inspired by Zoë and Jordan, Episode 3: Diagon Alley

For the Cakes

6½ ounces (185 ml) light olive oil

3 large eggs

1½ cups (300 g) granulated sugar

Zest and juice of 2 lemons

2 cups (250 g) all-purpose flour

½ teaspoon baking powder

½ teaspoon baking soda

1 tablespoon rosemary leaves, finely chopped

1 tablespoon thyme leaves, finely chopped

For the Raspberry Jelly

1 pound (455 g) raspberries

⅔ cup (150 g) superfine sugar

2 tablespoons water

3 super premium or platinum grade gelatin leaves

6 tablespoons (90 g) smooth raspberry jam

For the Lemon Mousse

Zest and juice of 2 lemons

¼ cup (55 g) superfine sugar

7 tablespoons water

4 super premium or platinum grade gelatin leaves

1¼ cups (300 ml) heavy cream

For the White Chocolate Glaze

17½ ounces (495 g) white chocolate, chopped

½ cup (120 g) coconut oil

Blue, green, and red food coloring

Fondant decorations (optional)

Prep time: 1 hour 15 minutes, plus cooling and chilling time

Cook time: 35 minutes

Flourish and Blotts, Diagon Alley's famous bookshop, is crammed with books of the wizarding world. This recipe is inspired by Zoë and Jordan's lemony, herbal book cakes. Losing by only one vote, these very nearly won the task. Like the hidden mysteries of the books themselves, the delicious flavors in these cakes are revealed only once they are opened.

TO MAKE THE CAKES

1. Preheat the oven to 350°F (180°C). Prepare a 12-by-8-inch springform baking pan by greasing the base and sides and lining with parchment paper.

2. Whisk the olive oil, eggs, granulated sugar, and lemon zest and juice in a large mixing bowl. Fold through the flour, baking powder, baking soda, rosemary, and thyme until well combined. Transfer the batter to the prepared pan and level the surface. Bake for 30 to 35 minutes, until risen, golden brown, and a skewer inserted in the middle comes out clean. Leave to cool completely in the pan. Once cooled, remove the sides of the pan and use a serrated bread knife to trim about ¼ inch off the top layer to level it, reserving any offcuts and keeping it on the parchment paper.

TO MAKE THE JELLY

1. Add the raspberries, superfine sugar, and water to a saucepan. Cover with a lid and cook over medium heat, stirring occasionally, until really soft (6 to 8 minutes). Meanwhile, soak the gelatin leaves in a bowl of cold water for 5 minutes.

2. Pour the raspberries into a fine-mesh sieve over a bowl and use the back of a ladle to press out as much liquid as possible. Discard the seeds and pulp. Return the liquid to the saucepan, squeeze the gelatin to remove excess water, and add the gelatin to the pan, stirring over low heat until melted, being sure not to boil it. Transfer to a cup with a spout and top up with cold water to make 1½ cups (360 ml).

3. Return the cake to the pan, with the parchment paper, and tightly wrap the outside of the cake pan with plastic wrap to catch any jelly that might leak. Use the cake offcuts to plug any gaps between the cake and the sides of the pan, then spread the raspberry jam in a thin layer over the top of the cake, covering any gaps. The jam will create a seal to prevent the jelly from leaking around the cake while setting. Carefully pour the jelly over the jam layer. Chill until set (4 hours, or overnight).

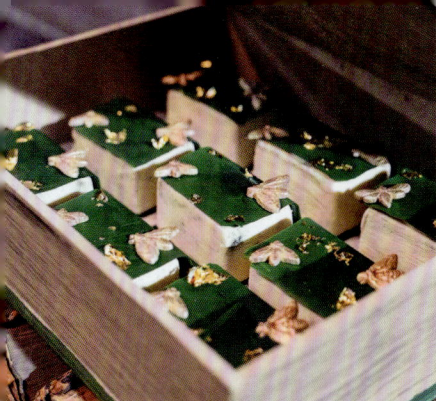

TO MAKE THE LEMON MOUSSE

1. Place the lemon zest, juice, superfine sugar, and water in a saucepan over low heat and stir until the sugar has dissolved. Turn up the heat and gently simmer until slightly syrupy (2 minutes). Set aside. Meanwhile, soak the gelatin leaves in a bowl of cold water for 5 minutes. Squeeze to remove excess water, then add the gelatin to the pan and cook, stirring, over low heat until melted. Transfer to a cup with a spout and set aside to cool.

2. In a large bowl with a handheld mixer, or in a stand mixer, whip the cream to medium-stiff peaks. Whisk in the cooled lemon mixture and whisk again until it has thickened up. Spread this over the top of the jelly and smooth to level the surface. Chill in the fridge until set, for at least 4 hours or ideally overnight.

CONTINUED

Zoë and Jordan's Flourish and Blotts–themed showpiece (above and below), as seen in the show

Olive Oil, Rosemary, Lemon, and Thyme Book Cakes

Continued

TO MAKE THE GLAZE AND DECORATE

1. Once fully set, cut the cake into 12 rectangles, each one approximately 1½ by 4 inches. Line a baking sheet with parchment paper and set a wire rack on top of it, with the cakes on the rack. The parchment will catch the excess chocolate as you begin to decorate your book cakes.

2. Turn each cake cuboid on its side, so that the layer of cake is now on the left, with the layer of mousse on the right, making sure there is space between each of them.

3. Add the chocolate and coconut oil to a heatproof bowl set over a pan of barely simmering water, stirring until completely melted. Divide among three bowls and add the blue food coloring to the first, green to the second, and red to the third, adding more food coloring as needed until you reach the color strength that you want.

4. Carefully pour each color over four cake slices, so you have an even number of each. Use an angled palette knife to disperse each evenly all over the sides, resulting in four smooth blue, green, and red cakes.

5. Chill until firm but not completely solid (10 to 15 minutes). Carefully remove the cakes from the wire rack. Place them with the uncovered end facing to the right, like a book. Decorate the tops with fondant decorations, if desired.

> "Famous Harry Potter. Can't even go into a bookshop without making the front page!"
>
> —Draco Malfoy, *Harry Potter and the Chamber of Secrets* film

Jordan assembles his book cakes (left); the end result as shown on screen (right)

Jordan's
Rosemary and Thyme Olive Oil Cake

For a quicker bake that doesn't include mousse, try this. It's the recipe that Jordan used to create the brilliant book cakes in *Wizards of Baking* Task 4.

For the Cake

5½ cups (680 g) all-purpose flour

4¼ cups (854 g) granulated sugar

2 teaspoons salt

1½ teaspoons baking soda

1½ teaspoons baking powder

2¾ cups (660 ml) milk

8 eggs

½ cup and 1 tablespoon (135 ml) orange juice

3¼ cups (780 ml) olive oil

4 teaspoons thyme, minced

3 tablespoons rosemary, minced

For the Raspberry Rose Gelée

1 tablespoon gelatin

3 tablespoons water

2 cups (500 g) raspberry purée

½ cup (100 g) granulated sugar

½ cup (10 g) dried rose petals

Prep time: 45 minutes, plus cooling and chilling time

Cook time: 30 minutes

TO MAKE THE CAKE

1. Preheat the oven to 350°F (180°C). Grease the base and sides of two 9–inch baking pans, and line them with parchment paper. The cake batter should fill three-quarters of each pan.

2. In a medium bowl, mix the flour, granulated sugar, salt, baking soda, and baking powder.

3. In a large bowl, whisk together the milk, eggs, orange juice, and olive oil. Slowly add the dry ingredients to the wet ingredients and mix until incorporated. Fold in the thyme and rosemary.

4. Pour the batter into the prepared baking pans and bake for 30 to 35 minutes, or until a skewer inserted into the cake comes out clean. Leave to cool.

TO MAKE THE RASPBERRY ROSE GELÉE

1. Bloom the gelatin in a bowl with the water. Heat the purée and granulated sugar in a pot over medium heat until the sugar is dissolved. Turn off the heat, add the dried rose petals, and steep for 15 to 20 minutes.

2. Strain out the rose petals. Melt the gelatin in a heatproof bowl in the microwave and slowly add it to the warm purée. Stir to combine and let cool. When cool, spread the gelée over the cake and refrigerate until set.

ORIGINAL SHOW RECIPE!

Quality Quidditch Cake Pops

Inspired by *Wizards of Baking*, Episode 3: Diagon Alley

For the Brownie Cake

6 tablespoons (90 g) butter

2 ounces (55 g) unsweetened chocolate, broken up into small pieces

1 cup (200 g) sugar

2 eggs

¾ cup (95 g) all-purpose flour

For the Cake Pops

5 ounces (140 g) caramel bits

1 tablespoon water

12 to 14 long pretzel rods

15 ounces (425 g) semisweet chocolate melting wafers

One 11-ounce (310-g) bag butterscotch chips

Prep time: 1 hour, plus cooling and chilling time

Cook time: 30 minutes

Elizabeth and Juan's showpiece in Task 3 was based around Diagon Alley's famous sporting emporium, Quality Quidditch Supplies. Their immaculate showpiece presented edible Golden Snitches to maximum effect. For an easier Quidditch-themed bake, consider these tasty broomsticks. A delectable blend of sweet and salty, this brownie-based cake pop is sculpted to look like your favorite form of wizarding transport.

TO MAKE THE BROWNIE CAKE

1. Preheat the oven to 350°F (180°C). Line an 8-by-8-inch baking pan with parchment paper, allowing it to overhang slightly.

2. In a large microwave-safe bowl, microwave the butter and chocolate together in 10-second increments, stirring in between bursts. When the chocolate is completely melted and the mixture is smooth, add the sugar, stirring to incorporate. Add the eggs one at a time, mixing thoroughly after each addition. Add the flour and stir until totally incorporated.

3. Pour the batter into the prepared pan and bake for 25 to 30 minutes, or until a cake tester comes out clean or with only a few crumbs. Allow to cool for 15 minutes, then use the parchment paper to lift the brownie from the pan. Refrigerate for 30 minutes or overnight.

TIP

These can be stored in an airtight container separated by parchment paper for 3 to 5 days. Or they can be packaged in cellophane bags to give as favors.

TO MAKE THE CAKE POPS

1. In a microwave-safe bowl or measuring cup, microwave the caramel and water together in short increments, stirring in between, until completely melted.

2. In a large bowl, use a wooden spoon to break up the brownie into an even, coarse-crumb texture. Add the melted caramel and stir until well combined. Refrigerate for 30 minutes.

3. Prepare two cookie sheets with baking mats or parchment paper. Have your pretzel rods close at hand.

4. Working with about 3 tablespoons of chilled brownie mixture, use your hands to form a thick patty out of the crumb mix and place a pretzel rod about halfway through the center of the top of it. Close the brownie mixture around the rod and shape the remaining portion into the "bristle" section of the broom. Gently press the bottom of the broom onto the cookie sheet, creating a flat bottom. Lay the broom down.

5. Repeat with the remaining pretzels and brownie mixture. Then, freeze the broom pops for 30 minutes.

6. In a medium microwave-safe bowl, microwave the semisweet chocolate in short bursts. Stir frequently, and be careful not to overheat.

7. Dip each frozen broom pop into the melted chocolate. Use a spatula to gently coat the entire "bristle" portion. Make sure to get chocolate on the joint between the pretzel and the brownie mixture to seal the cake pop to the pretzel rod. Shake the pop gently over the bowl to remove excess chocolate, and set the flat bottom back on the cookie sheet, so the broom is now standing.

8. Repeat with the remaining brooms until they are all coated in the chocolate. Save any remaining chocolate and set aside.

9. In another microwave-safe bowl, microwave the butterscotch chips in short bursts, being careful not to overheat.

10. Use a pastry brush (silicone works best) to brush the melted butterscotch chips onto the cake portion of each broom pop. Work slowly in long strokes, and let the lines show to create a bristle texture. Repeat with all the broom pops.

11. If necessary, gently reheat the semisweet chocolate. Fill a pastry bag with the chocolate, snip a small hole in the end, and pipe the broom bands onto each brownie pop. Allow 10 to 15 minutes to set.

Wand Box Cakes

Inspired by Hemu and Riccardo, Episode 3: Diagon Alley

For the Coconut Dacquoise
¾ cup (70 g) desiccated coconut

2 ounces (55 g) powdered sugar

1 tablespoon cornstarch

3 large egg whites

½ cup (110 g) superfine sugar

For the Raspberry Mousse
10½ ounces (300 g) raspberries

¼ cup (55 g) superfine sugar

2 tablespoons water

4 super premium or platinum grade gelatin leaves

1¼ cups (300 ml) heavy cream

1 teaspoon vanilla extract

For the Raspberry Jelly
1 pound (455 g) raspberries

¼ cup (55 g) superfine sugar

2 tablespoons water

3 super premium or platinum grade gelatin leaves

For the Chocolate Mousse
5½ ounces (155 g) dark chocolate

4 large eggs, separated

⅓ cup (75 g) superfine sugar

3 super premium or platinum grade gelatin leaves

1¼ cups (300 ml) heavy cream

For the Chocolate Glaze
17½ ounces (495 g) dark chocolate, chopped

½ cup (120 g) coconut oil

Edible blue glitter spray

Prep time: 2 hours,
plus cooling and chilling time

Cook time: 1 hour

With coconut, raspberry, and dark chocolate, this recipe retains the spirit of Hemu and Riccardo's delicious entremet wand boxes (pictured right). On screen, the pair used a mold to shape their raspberry gelée, coconut dacquoise, raspberry mousse, and vanilla raspberry mousseline sponges encased in chocolate, but this recipe offers a slightly simpler take while retaining the same flavor profiles.

TO MAKE THE COCONUT DACQUOISE

1. Preheat the oven to 300°F (150°C). Prepare a 12-by-8-inch springform baking pan by greasing the base and sides and lining with parchment paper.

2. Add the desiccated coconut to a small frying pan over medium heat and cook, stirring, for 2 to 3 minutes, until light brown and smelling nutty. Transfer to a bowl to cool completely, then stir through the powdered sugar and cornstarch.

3. Add the egg whites to a large mixing bowl and use a handheld electric mixer or stand mixer with the whisk attachment to whisk the egg whites for 4 to 5 minutes, until they form stiff peaks. Gradually whisk the superfine sugar in, a tablespoon at a time, until you have a really thick, glossy mixture. Gently fold through the coconut mixture until evenly combined, then spoon into the prepared pan and smooth to level it. Bake for 1 hour, then turn the oven off and leave in the oven for a further hour. Remove from the oven and leave to cool completely.

TO MAKE THE RASPBERRY MOUSSE

1. Add the raspberries, superfine sugar, and water to a saucepan, cover with a lid, and cook over medium heat, stirring occasionally, until really soft, 6 to 8 minutes. Meanwhile, soak the gelatin leaves in a bowl of cold water for 5 minutes.

2. Once the raspberries are cooked, set a fine-mesh sieve over a bowl and pour the raspberries into the sieve, then use the back of a ladle to press them through, ensuring you get as much liquid out as possible. Discard the seeds and pulp in the sieve. Return the liquid to the saucepan, squeeze the gelatin to remove excess water, then add it to the pan and cook, stirring, over low heat until the gelatin has melted. Make sure not to boil the gelatin. Transfer the mixture to a cup with a spout and set aside to cool.

3. Add the cream and vanilla to a mixing bowl and use a handheld electric whisk to whip the cream, until you have stiff peaks. Whisk in the raspberry mixture. Place the dacquoise on a wire rack set over a baking sheet and then pour the mousse over the dacquoise, making sure it reaches the edges. Don't worry if the mixture looks slightly runny at this stage, as it will firm up as it chills. Chill in the fridge until firm, at least 4 hours.

CONTINUED

CAKE INSPIRATION!

Hemu and Riccardo's stunning wand box cakes, pictured here, were made using molds. Our simplified recipe doesn't call for this, but you could mimic the beautiful presentation they used by presenting your versions on gold cake boards and adding a fondant tie.

Wand Box Cakes

Continued

❋

TO MAKE THE JELLY

1. Add the raspberries, superfine sugar, and water to a saucepan. Cover with a lid and cook over medium heat, stirring occasionally, until really soft (6 to 8 minutes). Meanwhile, soak the gelatin leaves in a bowl of cold water for 5 minutes.

2. Pour the raspberries into a fine-mesh sieve over a bowl and use the back of a ladle to press out as much liquid as possible. Discard the seeds and pulp and return the liquid to the saucepan. Squeeze the gelatin to remove excess water. Add the gelatin to the pan and cook, stirring, over low heat until melted, being sure not to boil it. Transfer to a cup with a spout and top up with cold water to make 1½ cups (360 ml).

3. Pour this over the set mousse and chill for at least 4 hours until set.

"The wand chooses the wizard, Mr. Potter.
It's not always clear why. But I think it is clear
that we can expect great things from you."

—Garrick Ollivander,
Harry Potter and the Sorcerer's Stone film

❋

TO MAKE THE CHOCOLATE MOUSSE

1. Melt the chocolate in a heatproof bowl set over a pan of barely simmering water. Meanwhile, add the egg yolks and superfine sugar to a mixing bowl and whisk using a handheld electric mixer or stand mixer with the whisk attachment until pale and fluffy (2 to 3 minutes). Soak the gelatin leaves in a bowl of cold water for 5 minutes.

2. Add ¼ cup (60 ml) cream to a small saucepan, then squeeze the excess water out of the gelatin and add the gelatin to the cream. Heat over low heat, stirring constantly, until the gelatin has melted, ensuring it doesn't boil. Add the melted chocolate and gelatin mixture to the egg yolk mixture and stir well. In a separate bowl, whisk the remaining 1 cup (240 ml) cream to medium-stiff peaks. Fold this through the chocolate mixture.

3. Add the egg whites to a separate mixing bowl and whisk until they have formed stiff peaks. Using a large metal spoon, take a third of the egg white mixture and vigorously mix it into the chocolate mixture to loosen it slightly, then gently fold through the remaining egg whites. Pour this over the set jelly and spread to level it, then chill for at least 4 hours until firm.

4. Once the chocolate mousse has fully set, slice the dacquoise into 12 rectangles, each approximately 1½ by 4 inches. Line a baking sheet with parchment paper and set a wire rack on top of it. This is intended to catch any excess chocolate at the decorating stage. Lay your dacquoise pieces on the wire rack, making sure there is space between each.

TO MAKE THE CHOCOLATE GLAZE

1. Add the chocolate and coconut oil to a heatproof bowl set over a pan of barely simmering water and stir until completely melted. Transfer to a cup with a spout and carefully pour this over the dacquoise slices, using an angled palette knife to spread all over the sides. Chill until firm but not completely solid (10 to 15 minutes).

2. Carefully remove the dacquoise cakes from the wire rack and spray with the blue glitter. Hemu and Riccardo added a chocolate wand to the top of each before decorating with a fondant tie.

FORBIDDEN FOREST

DARK
DELIGHTS

The chefs branch out with Forbidden flavors.

Professor Dumbledore's first instruction to the Hogwarts first years in the *Harry Potter and the Sorcerer's Stone* film is that the Dark Forest is strictly forbidden to all students. It's clearly not a rule that Harry takes on board, as he visits it almost every year he is at the school. The *Wizards of Baking* chefs also became acquainted with the Forest, as it provided the location for their fourth task. They had to think big, as their showpiece needed to be at least three feet tall and contain a tasting element with a minimum of ten layers.

Harry's first visit to the Dark Forest, also known as the Forbidden Forest, is to serve detention with Hermione, Ron, and Draco. When the Slytherin student expresses concern that there are werewolves in the Forest, school caretaker Argus Filch helpfully points out that the trees conceal much more. For the *Harry Potter and the Sorcerer's Stone* film, a combination of location and studio shooting was used to create the Forest. In *Harry Potter and the Chamber of Secrets*, the Forest was moved entirely inside for the scenes when Harry and Ron meet Aragog. This fearsome creature was built as a model, rather than created digitally. It was cable-controlled with water pumped through air rams instead of oil, giving Aragog a slow, menacing gait. Although the four remaining *Wizards of Baking* teams didn't have to face down a horde of hungry Acromantula when they presented their latest desserts at Leavesden, they were watched over by another resident of the Forbidden Forest, a Hippogriff called Buckbeak. In *Harry Potter and the Prisoner of Azkaban*, Rubeus Hagrid introduces this majestic beast to his students. Looking like a cross between a horse and an eagle, Buckbeak proved a challenge for the filmmakers. The creature effects department created a life-size model that would be used in some shots. The "bird" half of the Hippogriff proved the more difficult of the two, as each feather had to be individually inserted and glued, with some still being added on the first day the model was needed on set. The *Wizards of Baking* chefs also had to work up until the last second to realize their visions—with equally impressive results.

✳ Miko and Chris

In the *Harry Potter and the Prisoner of Azkaban* movie, Hogwarts plays host to the terrifying Dementors. Miko's version is unlikely to consume anyone's soul but is likely to be consumed itself, being made from tasty chocolate cake with chocolate ganache, mango filling, and mango buttercream frosting. Chris's grassy hill is a reverse Black Forest cake, featuring cherry cake, milk chocolate ganache, tarragon-poached cherries, and torched homemade marshmallow.

Zoë and Jordan

Before Dolores Umbridge is dragged away by centaurs into the Forbidden Forest, she is responsible for many dark deeds in her office. Zoë and Jordan's London fog crêpe cake pays tribute to the scene when Harry is punished while his teacher sips tea. The licorice and blackcurrant macarons have a feminine aesthetic with a black center, just like Professor Umbridge!

Lisa and Mitzi

Arachnophobes should avoid the Forbidden Forest, but this roller-skating spider is not what it appears—it's a Boggart. Inspired by the scene in *Harry Potter and the Prisoner of Azkaban* when Ron confronts his worst fear, the body is layered Mexican cake, packed with different fruit flavors. The spider's eyes are white chocolate shells filled with strawberry jam, candied sesame seeds, and strawberry marshmallow.

✴ Elizabeth and Juan

Inky black faces of Lord Voldemort are encircled by Nagini, made from modeling chocolate, in Elizabeth and Juan's unsettling design. Representing the darkness within Lord Voldemort, their creation also features four more Horcruxes appearing to float inside the faces— Marvolo Gaunt's ring, Helga Hufflepuff's cup, Rowena Ravenclaw's diadem, and Salazar Slytherin's locket. Tom Riddle's diary and rice paper "tendrils" complete the dessert.

CREATURE COMFORTS

The Forbidden Forest provides sanctuary to a curious collection of creatures, including Acromantula, Thestrals, and centaurs. For the fourth *Wizards of Baking* task, it was also home to eight talented chefs, as they took inspiration from this mystical location for their fantastic desserts.

Miko and Chris (above far left) fashioned a Dementor from a double barrel chocolate cake, rising above a foggy lake. Although this haunting scene might not look like it is filled with joy, it was! Miko's favorite fruit is mango, which was used for the cake's filling and buttercream frosting. Just like a Patronus bringing comfort and positive thoughts to ward off a Dementor, this is the pleasing effect that mango has on Miko. Chris feels happy when he is making or eating his favorite Black Forest dessert, which was the basis for the ten-layer entremet hill.

Elizabeth (above left) and Juan highlighted Horcruxes with their Nagini cake. Two of these pieces of Lord Voldemort's soul formed the tasting elements. The jewels on the Ravenclaw diadem were black sesame praline and mascarpone ganache bonbons. Tom Riddle's diary was a layered black velvet cake with mint buttercream. Both bakers used strong colors to represent the darkness of Lord Voldemort's pursuit of immortality, with the bright green buttercream representing the Dark Mark.

FRUITS OF THE FOREST

By contrast, Zoë (below) and Jordan's design prioritized pink over pitch black, and a cute cat instead of a creepy creature. However, with Dolores Umbridge as its inspiration, it wasn't lacking in the fear factor! The bakers' multilayered crêpe cake (page 76) had deeper Earl Grey flavors at the bottom, with frothed milk toward the top. Notes of lavender and honey recalled the sugary sweet appearance of Professor Umbridge's office and the persona she presents, disguising her true sour nature. The blackcurrant and licorice macarons played on a flavor combination found in British sweets.

Mitzi and Lisa (below left) know that laughter defeats a Boggart, so they infused their creation with joy—from its comical appearance to their favorite flavors. The Mexican cake contained guava jam, mango passion fruit crémeux, whipped coconut ganache, and cucumber lime gelée, reminding Lisa of the fruit stands she visited when she was growing up. *Fresas con crema*, or strawberries and cream, is the favorite dessert of Mitzi's mom, so those flavors feature in the spider's eyes. Sadly for Mitzi and Lisa, their Boggart bake didn't leave the judges overjoyed, as it proved their turn to leave the contest. Miko and Chris were declared the winners—with their Black Forest–style cake appropriately taking the plaudits in the Dark Forest.

Jordan's Blackcurrant Macarons and Earl Grey Crêpe Cake

From *Wizards of Baking*, Episode 4: Forbidden Forest

For the Macarons

4¼ cups (500 g) powdered sugar

5 cups (500 g) almond flour

10 egg whites (340 g)

2½ cups (500 g) granulated sugar

¼ cup (60 ml) water

Food coloring (optional)

For the Blackcurrant Fruit Leather

1¾ cups (450 g) blackcurrant purée

¼ cup (50 g) granulated sugar

1 tablespoon lemon juice

For the Black Licorice Gel

½ cup (100 g) muscovado sugar

½ cup (120 ml) water

1½ tablespoons orange juice

¾ ounce (21 g) licorice purée

1 teaspoon molasses

2 teaspoons lemon juice

2 teaspoons agar agar

For the Blackcurrant Ganache

2 cups (500 g) blackcurrant purée

1 pound and 1½ ounces (500 g) white chocolate

Special Equipment

Silicone baking mat

Prep time: 1 hour, plus cooling and chilling time

Cook time: 40 minutes

Afternoon tea with Dolores Umbridge might have included the flavors of blackcurrant and Earl Grey, which both feature here. The Professor also had a penchant for slipping Veritaserum into her guests' tea—thankfully, that truth-telling potion is omitted from Jordan's list of ingredients!

TO MAKE THE MACARONS

1. Preheat the oven to 280°F (137°C). Line a half sheet pan with a silicone baking mat.

2. Blend the powdered sugar and almond flour in a food processor until fine. Add half of the egg whites to the sugar and flour. Mix with a rubber spatula until a paste forms.

3. Place the granulated sugar and water in a medium pot and bring to 250°F (121°C). As the sugar heats up, put the remaining egg whites in a bowl of a stand mixer fitted with a whisk attachment and whip on medium speed until frothy. Add food coloring if wanted. When the sugar is at temperature, reduce the mixer speed to low and slowly pour the sugar into the mixer bowl. Once all the sugar is added, turn the mixer to high and whip until cool.

4. When the egg white mixture is cool, add to the paste in three increments, folding until fully incorporated each time. Place the mixture in a piping bag with a medium round tip. Pipe onto the baking mat, about a half dollar in size. Bake for 11 minutes. Allow to cool. Remove the macarons from the baking mat, then wrap and store at room temperature.

TO MAKE THE BLACKCURRANT FRUIT LEATHER

1. Preheat the oven to 200°F (95°C) and line a baking sheet with a silicone baking mat.

2. In a medium bowl, mix all the ingredients together. Spread on the prepared baking sheet and bake for 20 to 30 minutes, or until the purée is dry. Remove from the oven and let cool.

TO MAKE THE BLACK LICORICE GEL

1. Mix all the ingredients together in a pot and bring to a boil. Pour into a medium heatproof bowl and let set in the fridge for about 30 minutes.

2. Once fully set, using a handheld electric mixer or an immersion blender, whip until the gel is fully loose and a pipable consistency.

TO MAKE THE BLACKCURRANT GANACHE AND ASSEMBLE

1. Bring the purée to a boil in a pan over medium-high heat. Pour over the white chocolate in a heatproof bowl and mix until emulsified. Allow to set before use.

2. Find two macaron shells that match in size. Using a small round piping tip, pipe a ring of ganache on the bottom of one shell, leaving room in the middle to pipe the licorice gel. Place the second macaron shell on top, bottom side down. Stick fruit leather to the top of each sandwiched macaron with a little kiss of ganache. Allow to set.

ORIGINAL SHOW RECIPE!

Jordan also added a chocolate collar to his impressive crêpe cake

For the Earl Grey Crêpes

1 cup (227 g) butter, melted

16 eggs

Seeds from 4 vanilla beans

5¾ cups (720 g) all-purpose flour

½ cup (100 g) granulated sugar

2 teaspoons salt

4 tablespoons Earl Grey tea leaves

1 cup (240 ml) warm water

6 cups (1.44 L) milk

2 tablespoons lavender oil

For the Vanilla Mousse

1½ tablespoons gelatin

5 tablespoons water

2⅔ cups (630 ml) heavy cream

1 vanilla bean

12 ounces (340 g) white chocolate

For the Lavender Mascarpone Cream

4 ounces (115 g) mascarpone

½ cup (110 g) granulated sugar

1 cup minus 1 tablespoon (225 ml) heavy cream

1 tablespoon lavender oil

For the Mirror Glaze

3 tablespoons gelatin

2⅓ cups (560 ml) water

1½ cups (500 g) glucose

2½ cups (500 g) granulated sugar

3½ ounces (100 g) white chocolate

¾ cup (160 g) cocoa butter

1 cup (320 g) condensed milk

Prep time: 1 hour
plus cooling and chilling time

Cook time: 40 minutes

TO MAKE THE EARL GREY CRÊPES

1. Place all the ingredients in a blender and blend until smooth (you may need to do this in batches and then combine the batches in a large bowl). Let the batter sit in the refrigerator overnight. Strain out the Earl Grey tea leaves.

2. Spray a nonstick pan before each use. Heat the pan over medium heat. Pour a small amount of batter into the hot pan, swirl to coat the bottom, fry until golden brown in places (about 1 minute), then flip over to fry the other side. Slide the crêpe out of the pan onto a plate and repeat until all the batter is used, stacking the crêpes as you go.

TO MAKE THE VANILLA MOUSSE

1. In a small bowl, bloom the gelatin in the water. Place 1 cup and 14 tablespoons (450 ml) of the cream in a large bowl and whip with a handheld electric mixer until soft peaks form. Place the remaining ¾ cup (180 ml) cream and the vanilla bean in a pan and bring to a boil over medium-high heat. With a slotted spoon, remove the vanilla bean.

2. Place the white chocolate and bloomed gelatin in a heatproof bowl, pour over the hot cream, and mix until emulsified. Slowly fold in the soft whipped cream.

3. The mousse can be piped onto the finished crêpe cake or frozen in molds. Place the mousse in a piping bag and pipe into any silicone mold of your choice. Place in the freezer until solid. Remove and temper for 2 to 4 hours before eating.

TO MAKE THE LAVENDER MASCARPONE CREAM AND ASSEMBLE

1. Place the mascarpone and granulated sugar in the bowl of a stand mixer fitted with a paddle attachment and whip until smooth. Using a whisk attachment, slowly add the cream and whisk until smooth. Whip until medium peaks form. Fold in the lavender oil

2. Layer the crêpes with the cream to the desired thickness. Place the cake on a wire rack set over a baking sheet.

TO MAKE THE MIRROR GLAZE

1. In a small bowl, bloom the gelatin with ⅔ cup (160 ml) of the water. Bring the glucose, granulated sugar, and 1 cup (240 ml) of the water to a boil in a large pot.

2. Place the white chocolate, cocoa butter, bloomed gelatin, and remaining ⅔ cup (160 ml) of water in a large heatproof bowl. Pour the hot glucose mixture over the chocolate mixture. Mix until combined. Lastly, mix in the condensed milk. Pour the glaze over the top of the cake.

Skull Cakes

Inspired by *Wizards of Baking*, Episode 4: Forbidden Forest

Butter or oil, for greasing

2 cups (250 g) all-purpose flour

1 cup and 2 teaspoons (105 g) cocoa powder

1 tablespoon baking powder

1 teaspoon kosher salt

1½ cups (340 g) unsalted butter, softened

1 cup (200 g) granulated sugar

⅔ cup (135 g) light brown sugar, packed

4 large eggs

1 tablespoon vanilla extract

¾ cup (180 ml) milk

½ cup (90 g) mini chocolate chips

2 teaspoons powdered sugar

Special Equipment

11.8-by-10-inch skull cakelet pan with six 2-inch-deep cavities

Prep time: 30 minutes, plus cooling time

Cook time: 35 minutes

Chocolate in the wizarding world isn't just for a snack or dessert—it's helpful after a Dementor encounter. Harry discovers this when Remus Lupin offers him some after a confrontation with these Dark creatures in the *Harry Potter and the Prisoner of Azkaban* film.

Inspired by Miko and Christopher's Dementor-themed showpiece from Task 4, these lush individual dark chocolate cakes are baked in special mini cake pans in the shape of a skull—a ghoulish reminder that no one wants to encounter a Dementor face to face.

1. Preheat the oven to 325°F (165°C). Grease the insides of the skull cakelet pan.

2. In a large mixing bowl, sift together the flour, 1 cup (100 g) of the cocoa powder, baking powder, and salt.

3. In the bowl of a stand mixer or a separate large bowl if using a hand mixer, cream together the butter, granulated sugar, and brown sugar until smooth and light brown, 2 to 3 minutes. Add the eggs one at a time, mixing well after each addition.

4. Stir together the vanilla and milk in a 1-cup measuring cup.

> "Here, eat this. It'll help.
> It's all right—it's chocolate."
>
> —Remus Lupin,
> *Harry Potter and the Prisoner of Azkaban* film

---

5. With the mixer running on its lowest setting, alternate between adding the milk mixture and adding the flour mixture into the butter mixture, until all has been added. Scrape down the sides of the bowl as needed, to ensure even mixing. Add the mini chocolate chips and blend to combine.

6. Fill each cakelet cavity about three-quarters full, tapping the pan to evenly distribute the batter. Bake for 30 to 35 minutes, until a skewer inserted into the center comes out clean.

7. Cool for 10 minutes and then invert onto a wire rack. Some cakelets may need a little loosening at the edges to come out.

8. Sift together the powdered sugar and remaining 2 teaspoons of cocoa powder in a small bowl. While still warm, dust the tops of the skull cakelets with the mixture.

Patronus Cake

Inspired by *Wizards of Baking*, Episode 4: Forbidden Forest

✳

For the Cake

3⅓ cups (415 g) all-purpose flour

2¼ teaspoons baking powder

¾ teaspoon baking soda

¼ teaspoon salt

1 cup (225 g) unsalted butter

2¼ cups (450 g) sugar

4 eggs

2 teaspoons vanilla extract

2 teaspoons lemon zest

½ cup (120 ml) lemon juice

1 cup (250 g) Greek yogurt

For the White Chocolate Mousse Filling

¾ teaspoon gelatin

3 tablespoons cold water

8 ounces (225 g) white chocolate

1½ cups (360 ml) heavy cream

For the Buttercream

⅔ cup (160 g) pasteurized egg whites

1½ cups (300 g) powdered sugar

2 cups (450 g) unsalted butter, softened, cut into tablespoon-size pieces

1 teaspoon vanilla extract

For Decorating

6 ounces (170 g) white chocolate

Sparkle sugar

Two 13½-ounce (380-g) containers pirouette cookies

Special Equipment

Stag and Doe Patronus Cake Topper templates (see page 91)

Prep time: 1 hour, plus cooling and chilling time

Cook time: 40 minutes

Decorated to look like the forest where Harry first sees the Doe Patronus in *Harry Potter and the Deathly Hallows–Part 1*, this stunning cake calls to mind that key scene and offers a lighter interpretation of a Forest-themed bake. There are no frightening Acromantula in this design!

TO MAKE THE CAKE

1. Preheat the oven to 350°F (180°C). Prepare two 8-inch cake pans by lining the bottom with parchment paper.

2. In a medium bowl, mix all the dry ingredients together. Set aside.

3. In the bowl of a stand mixer fitted with a paddle attachment, beat the butter and sugar until light and fluffy. Add in the eggs, one at a time, scraping down the sides after each addition. Add the vanilla and lemon zest. In a small bowl, mix the lemon juice with the Greek yogurt.

4. Starting with about a third of the dry mixture, alternate between adding the dry ingredients and the yogurt mixture to the bowl of the stand mixer. Mix well.

5. Divide the batter evenly between the two prepared pans. Bake for 30 to 35 minutes, or until a cake tester comes out clean. Allow the cakes to cool in the pan on a wire rack for 15 minutes, then turn out onto the wire rack to cool completely.

TO MAKE THE FILLING

1. In a small bowl, let the gelatin bloom in the cold water. Add the white chocolate to a medium heatproof bowl. In a small saucepan, heat ½ cup (120 ml) of the cream until just scalding, for 3 to 5 minutes. Add the gelatin mixture and stir until fully dissolved.

2. Pour the cream mixture over the white chocolate and allow to stand for 5 minutes. Stir to completely melt the chocolate.

3. In the bowl of a stand mixer fitted with a whisk attachment, whisk the remaining 1 cup (240 ml) of cream on high speed until stiff peaks form. Fold the white chocolate mixture into the whipped cream and chill for at least 2 hours.

CONTINUED

Patronus Cake

TO MAKE THE BUTTERCREAM

1. Place a heatproof measuring cup or bowl inside a saucepan. Fill the saucepan with water until the water level reaches halfway up the cup. Remove the measuring cup and turn the heat to medium. Bring the water to a simmer.

2. In the measuring cup, combine the egg whites with the powdered sugar and whisk until blended. Place the measuring cup into the simmering water and heat, stirring constantly, until the sugar is completely dissolved and the mixture is hot.

3. Carefully remove the measuring cup of sugar-egg mixture from the saucepan, and transfer the contents to the bowl of a stand mixer fitted with a whisk attachment. Whisk the egg white and sugar mixture on high until completely cool. It should be white and opaque—a loose, sticky meringue (7 to 10 minutes). Add the softened butter to the meringue with the mixer on low speed and mix until incorporated. Add the vanilla and turn up the mixer to medium; mix until smooth (1 to 2 minutes).

> "A full-bodied Patronus
> is the most difficult to produce,
> but shield forms can also be equally
> useful against a variety of opponents."
>
> —Harry Potter,
> *Harry Potter and the Order of the Phoenix* film

✳

TO ASSEMBLE AND DECORATE THE CAKE

1. Using a sharp knife, cut your cake rounds in half through the middle, creating four layers of cake.

2. Fill a pastry bag with a cup of buttercream. Cut an opening in the tip and have standing by. Working on a cake board or serving plate, smear a small amount of buttercream on the board and place the bottom layer of the cake over it. Use the piping bag to pipe a "wall" of buttercream around the edge of the layer. Fill with about a cup of chilled white chocolate mousse.

3. Repeat this process to create two more layers of cake and mousse. Place the fourth layer on top to finish the cake. Chill the cake for 30 minutes.

4. Using an offset spatula and the remaining buttercream, frost the entire cake. The sides will be covered in cookies, so it doesn't need to be perfect. At this point, the cake can be refrigerated for up to 24 hours. If the cake has been refrigerated, allow it to come to room temperature for 20 to 30 minutes before decorating.

5. Trace the Stag and Doe Patronus Cake Topper templates onto parchment paper.

6. In a microwave-safe bowl, melt the white chocolate in 30-second bursts, stirring between each one. Once the chocolate is melted, place it in a pastry bag.

7. Trace the stag and doe in the white chocolate and fill in. Sprinkle immediately with sparkle sugar. Drizzle the remaining white chocolate over all the pirouette cookies and sprinkle with more sparkle sugar. Allow to set for 5 to 10 minutes.

8. Press the cookies into the sides of the cake, breaking them at different lengths to create a staggered look. Once all the cookies are on the cake, scrape up the remaining chocolate and sugar from the parchment and sprinkle it on top of the cake.

9. Carefully remove the stag and doe from the parchment and use leftover cookie pieces to stand them up in the center of the cake.

Stag and Doe

Patronus Cake Topper
templates

Mandrake Cry Cupcakes

Inspired by *Wizards of Baking*, Episode 4: Forbidden Forest

For the Cupcakes

Cooking spray

1 cup (125 g) all-purpose flour

½ cup (100 g) granulated sugar

¼ cup (90 g) light brown sugar

1 teaspoon ground cinnamon

¼ teaspoon grated nutmeg

¼ teaspoon ground ginger

1 teaspoon baking soda

½ teaspoon baking powder

¼ teaspoon salt

1½ cups (75 g) grated carrots

⅔ cup (160 ml) canola oil

2 eggs, beaten

½ cup (65 g) chopped pecans

For the Frosting

8 ounces (225 g) cream cheese, softened

½ cup (115 g) unsalted butter, softened

3½ cups (420 g) powdered sugar

⅔ cup (65 g) unsweetened cocoa powder

1 teaspoon vanilla extract

1 to 2 tablespoons half-and-half

Pinch of salt

For Decorating

Brown gel food coloring

1 pound (455 g) white fondant

Chocolate sprinkles

Fresh mint sprigs

Special Equipment

12 small terra-cotta baking cups

Toothpicks or wooden skewer, cut into small pieces

Prep time: 1 hour, plus cooling time

Cook time: 14 minutes

There is no guarantee that you'd find a Mandrake in the Forbidden Forest, but these peculiar plants are such a memorable part of Herbology lessons at Hogwarts that they deserve to be included here. Garden-friendly carrot cake is matched with a rich chocolate cream cheese frosting and sprinkles to simulate soil. Finally, fondant Mandrakes with fresh mint leaves provide the perfect final touch.

TO MAKE THE CUPCAKES

1. Preheat the oven to 350°F (180°C). Lightly spray terra-cotta baking cups with cooking spray and set aside.

2. In a large bowl, combine the flour, sugars, spices, baking soda, baking powder, and salt.

3. Combine the grated carrots and the oil in a separate medium bowl. Slowly add the carrots to the flour mixture, stirring until just mixed. Add the eggs and pecans, and stir to gently combine.

4. Spoon the batter into the prepared baking cups, filling each approximately two-thirds full. Bake for 12 to 14 minutes, or until a toothpick comes out clean. Allow to cool completely before frosting.

> "The Mandrake's cry is fatal
> to anyone who hears it."
>
> —Hermione Granger,
> *Harry Potter and the Chamber of Secrets* film

TO MAKE THE FROSTING

1. In the bowl of a stand mixer fitted with a paddle attachment, beat the cream cheese and butter on medium speed until smooth (about 1 minute).

2. Add the powdered sugar, cocoa powder, vanilla, 1 tablespoon of half-and-half, and salt. Beat until creamy. Add more half-and-half if you need to thin the frosting. Using an offset spatula, apply a thin to medium layer of frosting to the cooled cupcakes.

TO MAKE THE DECORATIONS

1. Add a couple drops of brown gel food coloring to your fondant and knead the fondant to blend the color throughout. Add more coloring as needed to achieve your desired shade.

2. Divide the fondant into 12 pieces, approximately 3 by 4 inches, one for each of your Mandrakes. Working with one Mandrake at a time, tear off a third of the fondant and reserve it for the head. Tear another small amount from your remaining fondant and reserve this for the arms and roots.

3. With the remaining large piece of fondant, begin to roll and shape it into the Mandrake body—a roundish triangle with the wide part at the bottom. Press the bottom onto your surface so that you give your Mandrake a good base to sit on. Set aside.

4. Roll the headpiece into a ball, and adhere to the body with a toothpick or short piece of wooden skewer. Pull some "roots" up from the head and use a toothpick or skewer to create the eyes, mouth, and body texture. Poke a hole in the back of the head for the mint and two holes in the side of the body for the arms.

5. Roll the remaining piece into a long snake-like shape, and break it into four to five pieces so that you have two arms and a few pieces of roots to attach.

6. Connect the arms to the Mandrake, pinching to join the fondant pieces together. Wait to add the roots until the Mandrake is positioned on the cupcake.

7. Sprinkle the top of each cupcake with chocolate sprinkles. Alternatively, you can pour the sprinkles onto a plate and dip the top of each iced cupcake into them to create a smooth layer of sprinkles over the icing.

8. Place the Mandrake on top of the iced cupcake. If your Mandrake needs a little extra support, place a toothpick behind it in the cake to help stabilize it. Add the remaining roots to the base of the Mandrake and a sprig of fresh mint to the Mandrake's head where you placed the hole.

9. Repeat with the rest of the cupcakes and serve.

DUMBLEDORE'S OFFICE

CHOP AND CHANGE

The teams tackle a tricky transformation task.

The Harry Potter films afford the audience the opportunity to peer inside a number of teachers' rooms at Hogwarts. None of them are as filled with as many magical items as Professor Dumbledore's office. From the Sorting Hat, surveying the room from above an old bookcase, to the Sword of Gryffindor, which Harry uses to slay the Basilisk, the room is full of surprises for any student dispatched to see their headmaster. This meant a wealth of inspiration for the three remaining *Wizards of Baking* teams, who also had to include the theme of transformation and incorporate one sweet and sour combination and one salty and spicy flavor profile.

Albus Dumbledore's office is first seen in *Harry Potter and the Chamber of Secrets* after Harry is sent there, having been discovered close to the Petrified bodies of Justin Finch-Fletchley and Nearly Headless Nick. Production designer Stuart Craig and his team had the task of deciding on its appearance, as well as where it would be located in the castle. He recalls: "The most wonderful place is the aerie of a tower up above it all. So that was the beginning of his office—it came from the outside in."

Likewise, the *Wizards of Baking* chefs also had to think about the outward appearance of their amazing creations, although the flavor combinations contained inside were equally important.

Professor Dumbledore's office is also home to the Pensieve, which can be used to store memories. First seen in the *Harry Potter and the Goblet of Fire* film, this extraordinary magical device is used to view memories, such as the trial of Death Eater Igor Karkaroff. In this movie, the Pensieve is housed in a cabinet, but in *Harry Potter and the Half-Blood Prince*, the filmmakers decided to move the magical bowl from its sunken tabletop display and suspend it in midair instead.

The *Wizards of Baking* competitors were probably looking ahead, however, rather than concerning themselves with the past, as successfully navigating this task would be rewarded with a place in the final round!

Miko and Chris

On his first evening at Hogwarts in the *Harry Potter and the Sorcerer's Stone* film, Harry is amazed to see the portraits move. He would probably have been equally impressed by Miko and Chris's extraordinary cake for this task.

Hogwarts paintings aren't just for decoration. One guards the entrance to the Gryffindor common room, requiring a password to gain admittance. When Arthur Weasley is attacked by Nagini in *Harry Potter and the Order of the Phoenix*, pictures move between frames to ensure he is rescued. Miko's portrait isn't straightforward either, showing Professor Dumbledore, with his eyes closed, when seen from one side—and Professor Snape when viewed from the other. An appropriate subject for a sweet and sour theme, this double portrait cake combines yuzu and sherbet and features candied yuzu and yuzu custard.

The candles crafted by Chris provided the second tasting element. One of his signature styles involves modern takes on nostalgic flavors, which evoke memories when eaten. That is certainly the case with this PB&J layered dessert, which includes peanut butter mousse, Concord grape gelée, Oaxacan-spiced crumble, and chocolate-covered, spicy peanuts—a "light" snack bursting with taste!

✳ Elizabeth and Juan

Dumbledore's office is home to Fawkes the phoenix, recreated by Elizabeth and Juan for their fifth *Wizards of Baking* task. This astonishing bird is first seen in the *Harry Potter and the Chamber of Secrets* film, with the young wizard shocked to see him catch fire, before being reborn from the ashes. Acknowledging Fawkes's life cycle, the filmmakers chose to make his feathers the colors of flames. The bird's head is mainly burnt oranges and dark reds, while his underside is dominated by shades of gold. The chefs incorporated these colors into their dessert, as well as the flavor of the headmaster's favorite sweets!

The sweet and sour tasting element is Fawkes's body, which is Elizabeth's lemon sherbet cake. Like Professor Dumbledore, Elizabeth loves sherbet lemons and devoured them during her childhood in London. Here, she elevates that flavor profile with lemon velvet cake, lemon sweet cream, and pieces of sugary sour crunch.

Hidden in the ashes is Juan's spiced carrot cake. This is a nostalgic dessert for the chef and reminds him of watching the Harry Potter movies during the holidays with his partner. Mascarpone spiced mousse, salted caramel, and spicy pecan praline add extra depth, with the carrot cake also mimicking the colors of Fawkes.

✳ Zoë and Jordan

A trick dessert combines with a magical device used for trickery in Zoë and Jordan's fifth-round dessert. In the *Harry Potter and the Prisoner of Azkaban* film, a Time-Turner is given to Hermione so that she can attend two classes simultaneously. The chefs would undoubtedly also have appreciated being issued one, but they were still able to create their spectacular sculpture within the time limit.

The chefs' first tasting element is a deconstructed Bakewell tart in the shape of a lemon. Maintaining the theme of transformation, Zoë and Jordan's dessert looks completely different from how it tastes. Anyone expecting a sharp lemon tang will be pleasantly surprised as they bite into comforting Morello cherry mousse, almond frangipane, a cherry confit center, and almond sablé.

The Time-Turner theme forms the inspiration for their second component. Instead of creating a faithful reproduction, Zoë and Jordan wanted to evoke the spirit of the magical device, focusing on the instruments of time instead. Their two gold chocolate rings contain cream cheese mousse, ginger cake, miso caramel poached pears, and chocolate dip. It's definitely a dessert worth making time for!

FOOD FOR THOUGHTS

Albus Dumbledore's office is usually a serene sanctuary, where the headmaster collects his thoughts. For one night, it was a maelstrom of cakes, candies, and creams as the six *Wizards of Baking* chefs tended to their latest designs.

While Chris (above center right) perfected his impressive PB&J candles (above far right), Miko (below left) put his bachelor of fine arts major in painting to good use. His portrait of Albus Dumbledore and Severus Snape features two people that Miko credits, in particular, for helping Harry defeat Lord Voldemort.

Elizabeth and Juan (below right) presented a lustrous red and gold phoenix cake. Famously, on the set of *Harry Potter and the Chamber of Secrets*, Dumbledore actor Richard Harris thought that Fawkes was a real bird and wouldn't accept it was a model until it was brought to "life" at the touch of a button! Elizabeth and Juan's detailed cake might well have caused similar confusion.

With all three teams surpassing themselves, the judges had the challenging responsibility of choosing a winner. They selected Zoë (above left) and Jordan's deconstructed Time-Turner dessert (page 94)—the first time this team had finished in first place. Zoë was especially happy with the flavors that they had brought to the challenge. However, time had run out for Miko and Chris, as this proved to be their final contribution to the contest.

Jordan's Ginger Cake

From *Wizards of Baking*, Episode 5: Dumbledore's Office

For the Cake

½ cup (120 g) unsalted butter

1¾ cups (220 g) powdered sugar

¾ cup (80 g) almond flour

⅔ cup (80 g) all-purpose flour

½ teaspoon baking powder

5 tablespoons (30 g) ground ginger

6 egg whites (220 g)

For the Miso Caramel Pear

¾ cup (150 g) granulated sugar

1 cup (240 ml) heavy cream

1 vanilla bean, split and seeds scraped

Pinch of salt

2 tablespoons white miso paste

½ cup (100 g) diced pear

Prep time: 45 minutes, plus cooling time

Cook time: 35 minutes

The chocolate rings that made up part of Jordan and Zoë's task-winning Time-Turner were filled with different tastes and textures. Here are Jordan's recipes for two core elements of this creative concoction. The miso caramel pear can be used as a filling for the ginger cake or as a delicious dessert accompaniment.

TO MAKE THE CAKE

1. Preheat the oven to 350°F (180°C). Grease a 9-inch cake pan and line with parchment paper.

2. Place the butter in a medium pot and let it brown. In a stand mixer bowl fitted with a paddle attachment, paddle together the powdered sugar, flours, baking powder, and ginger.

3. Slowly add the egg whites until fully incorporated. Add the warmed brown butter and mix until smooth.

4. Spoon the batter into the prepared cake pan and bake for 30 to 35 minutes, or until a skewer inserted in the middle comes out clean. Let cool in the pan on a wire rack, then turn out the cake and let cool completely.

TO MAKE THE MISO CARAMEL PEAR

1. Place the granulated sugar in a large pot and cook until it is an amber caramel color. Slowly whisk in the cream until incorporated. Add the vanilla and salt. Add the miso paste and mix. Fold in the diced pears and let it cool. This can be served with the cake as a filling or spooned on top for a delicious dessert.

"This is a Time-Turner, Harry. McGonagall gave it to me first term. This is how I've been getting to my lessons all year."

—Hermione Granger,
Harry Potter and the Prisoner of Azkaban film

———— ✹ ————

Jordan's ginger cake and miso caramel pear recipes both featured in this episode's winning showpiece

Bakewell Pots with Lemony White Chocolate

Inspired by Zoë and Jordan, Episode 5: Dumbledore's Office

For the Frangipane

4¼ ounces (120 g) unsalted butter, softened

4¼ ounces (120 g) superfine sugar

1 large egg

½ teaspoon almond extract

1 tablespoon all-purpose flour

4¼ ounces (120 g) ground almonds

For the Cherry Mousse

7 ounces (200 g) pitted cherries, fresh or frozen (defrosted if frozen)

¼ cup (55 g) superfine sugar

1 tablespoon water

1 super premium or platinum grade gelatin leaf

1 cup (240 ml) heavy cream

10 tablespoons (205 g) smooth cherry jam

For the Almond Sablé Biscuits

7 ounces (200 g) unsalted butter, softened

¼ cup (55 g) superfine sugar

2 medium egg yolks

1 teaspoon almond extract

1 cup (125 g) all-purpose flour, plus more for dusting

½ cup (60 g) ground almonds

For the White Chocolate and Lemon Ganache

10½ ounces (300 g) white chocolate, chopped

¾ cup (180 ml) heavy cream

Zest of 1 lemon

Few drops of yellow food coloring

Special Equipment

Ten 2¾-inch (7-cm) ramekins

Prep time: 1 hour 10 minutes, plus cooling and chilling time

Cook time: 35 minutes

Of their "distorted sherbet lemons" showpiece component, Zoë and Jordan said: "In keeping with the theme of transformation, we wanted to make a dessert that looks like one thing but tastes completely like something else—tricking your brain into thinking it'll taste like something it's not."

This tasty dessert presents a similar idea without the need for a special mold and retains the flavor profiles presented: those of a classic British Bakewell tart, with a lemony white chocolate topping and crumbly almond sablé biscuits on the side.

TO MAKE THE FRANGIPANE

1. Preheat the oven to 350°F (180°C).

2. In a large mixing bowl, add the butter and superfine sugar and beat using a handheld electric mixer until pale (3 to 4 minutes). Add the egg and almond extract and beat well. Fold through the flour and ground almonds until well combined. Divide the mixture among 10 ramekins, placing about 1 tablespoon per ramekin, and use the back of a teaspoon to level the mixture. Place all the ramekins on a baking sheet and bake for 20 minutes, until the frangipane is light brown and cooked through, then set aside to cool completely.

TO MAKE THE CHERRY MOUSSE

1. Add the cherries, superfine sugar, and water to a saucepan and cook over medium heat until the cherries are very soft (8 to 10 minutes). Set aside to cool slightly, then transfer to a blender and blend until completely smooth. Meanwhile, add the gelatin leaf to a bowl of cold water and set aside to soak for 5 minutes.

2. In a medium bowl with a handheld mixer, whip the cream to soft peaks. Return the cherry purée to the pan, then squeeze excess water from the gelatin, add the gelatin to the pan, and cook over low heat, stirring, until just melted, making sure it doesn't boil. Transfer this mixture to a bowl and set aside to cool. Then, fold in the cream until evenly combined.

3. Top each frangipane ramekin with 1 tablespoon of the cherry jam. Then, divide the mousse among the ramekins and level the surface. Chill until the mousse is set (at least 2 hours).

TO MAKE THE ALMOND SABLÉ BISCUITS

1. Blend the butter and superfine sugar in a food processor until well combined. Add the remaining ingredients and whiz again until the mixture comes together. Transfer to a mixing bowl and knead the mixture lightly. Place the dough on a large piece of plastic wrap and shape into a roughly 1-centimeter-thick disk. Wrap well and chill until firm (about 45 minutes).

2. Once chilled, preheat the oven to 375°F (190°C) and line two large baking sheets with parchment paper.

3. Lightly dust your work surface and rolling pin with flour and roll the biscuit dough out to ⅛ inch thick. Using a 2½-inch round cutter, cut out twenty circles, then divide these between the baking sheets and bake for 10 to 12 minutes, until light brown and dry to the touch. Leave to cool completely on the baking sheets.

TO MAKE THE GANACHE AND SERVE

1. Add the white chocolate, cream, and lemon zest to a heatproof bowl set over a pan of barely simmering water, making sure the base doesn't touch the water. Stir until smooth and melted. Stir in a few drops of yellow food coloring until you have a deep yellow color. Allow to cool fully.

2. Spoon the ganache over the top of each ramekin, and place them back into the refrigerator until set (about 30 minutes). Serve with the sablé biscuits.

Zoë and Jordan's "distorted sherbet lemons" showpiece

THE
GREAT
HALL

FEAST
FINALE

Four creative chefs ... two like-minded teams ... one coveted trophy!

The Harry Potter films are brimming with fabulous food, from Chocolate Frogs and Bertie Bott's Every-Flavour Beans on the Hogwarts Express food trolley to dragon-roasted chestnuts from Diagon Alley. Some of the most mouthwatering meals are served at feasts in the Great Hall at Hogwarts School of Witchcraft and Wizardry. This proved to be the perfect location for the final round of *Wizards of Baking*, with the teams having already treated the judges to an array of incredible and inventive desserts. Elizabeth and Juan went head-to-head with Zoë and Jordan for the final baking battle.

The Great Hall appears in seven of the Harry Potter movies and is the setting for many iconic scenes. The audience is introduced to wizard chess there, with Ron demonstrating his skill at the game in *Harry Potter and the Sorcerer's Stone*. It is also the venue for Professor Lockhart's dueling demonstration, where Harry inadvertently reveals to the school that he can speak Parseltongue.

The massive room is based on a hall at Christ Church, University of Oxford in the UK and has almost the same dimensions, at 120 feet long and 40 feet wide. However, production designer Stuart Craig was not impressed by the windows in the original building. "So we elongated and lowered them," he reveals, "bringing the sills down to the three-foot level, so you could see out. And the roof at Christ Church was not quite up to our ambitions. So we went to the best medieval roof in this country, which, I think, is the hammer-beam one in Westminster Abbey, from the thirteenth century."

Four dining tables, one for each of the houses, fill the room. Often seen covered with enticing platters of food, these tables had to be specially made for the movies. Each table was 100 feet long, and the filmmakers were unable to find a place that would sell or rent such huge pieces of furniture, or the 800 feet of benches placed on either side of them.

For their final challenge, the chefs had to think big, too! They were tasked with creating a showpiece at least six feet tall that contained a magical element. As Professor Dumbledore once declared, "Let the feast begin!"

✳ Elizabeth and Juan

For their final challenge, Elizabeth and Juan recreated a famous scene from *Harry Potter and the Order of the Phoenix*, which had more to do with fun than feasting. Draconian teacher Professor Umbridge sits imperiously in the Great Hall, watching the fifth years struggle over their Theory of Charms O.W.L. The exams are interrupted, however, by Fred and George Weasley riding broomsticks and throwing magical fireworks around the room.

Fred and George drop out of school to open a joke shop on Diagon Alley, where they sell sweets far removed from anything served up on *Wizards of Baking*. The Weasleys' products cause illness, for anyone who wants a day off school. These include Puking Pastilles, which have a memorable dispenser in the film *Harry Potter and the Half-Blood Prince*. Concept artist Adam Brockbank explains: "We wanted to be funny and disgusting at the same time. So we came up with an idea based on charity boxes from the fifties. It was a slightly badly sculpted, six-foot-tall girl throwing up Puking Pastilles into a bucket."

Elizabeth and Juan are aiming for a more positive reaction from their dessert. Their list of ingredients includes dulce de leche, candy floss sugar, cookie butter, and dark chocolate— much more "yum" than "yuk."

Fred and George's frenetic firework display in the *Harry Potter and the Order of the Phoenix* film features a huge dragon head, which chases Professor Umbridge down the length of the Great Hall. Elizabeth's tasting element transforms the toothy beast into a toothsome treat. She describes her dragon dessert as having "Fancy Texas Turtle" flavors. Her chocolate whiskey cake contains pecan pie praline filling, bourbon caramel, and chocolate ganache. Elizabeth says: "I was inspired by the flavor and tradition of Texas cooking. Coming to America and feeling away from home, this flavor was the one that kept me close to my English upbringing."

As Professor Umbridge reaches the doorway in the movie, the fearsome firework beast crashes into the wall behind her. The newly appointed Hogwarts head's framed Educational Decrees are sent crashing to the floor, much to the delight of the students.

Juan's edible version of these awful orders consists of chocolate cake with coffee mousse, coffee caramel, and vanilla crémeux. The chef says: "I want to finish with a big moment that represents my flavors and where I am from. I want to do something that I know. This dessert is my favorite and is perfect for a finale. I also wanted to do the picture frames, as those are the rules Umbridge gave the students. They defied her, much like I am always trying to defy the norm when it comes to baking."

SILENCE
O.W.L. EXAMS
IN PROGRESS

✳ Zoë and Jordan

During his first year at Hogwarts, Harry spends the Christmas holidays at his new school, which is no doubt a more pleasing proposition than returning to the Dursley household. In the *Harry Potter and the Sorcerer's Stone* movie, the Great Hall was given the festive treatment by production designer Stuart Craig, with a wreath hanging on the doors and pine needle boughs placed over doorways. Eight Christmas trees lined the Hall, with a larger ninth tree standing behind the professors' high table. All the trees were lavishly decorated with gold-colored stars, crescent moons, and gilded globes. In the movie, Professor Flitwick gets the credit for the attractive arrangements, using the Levitation Charm to place the baubles.

For the final *Wizards of Baking* round, Zoë and Jordan pay tribute to Hogwarts's festive fare with their version of a roast turkey dinner sitting next to a decorated Christmas tree and a candelabra of cake candles. The chefs' dessert is packed full of seasonal flavors, with cinnamon, nutmeg, allspice, cardamom, cloves, and ginger featuring in their recipes. There is even a nip of brandy to add some extra winter warmth!

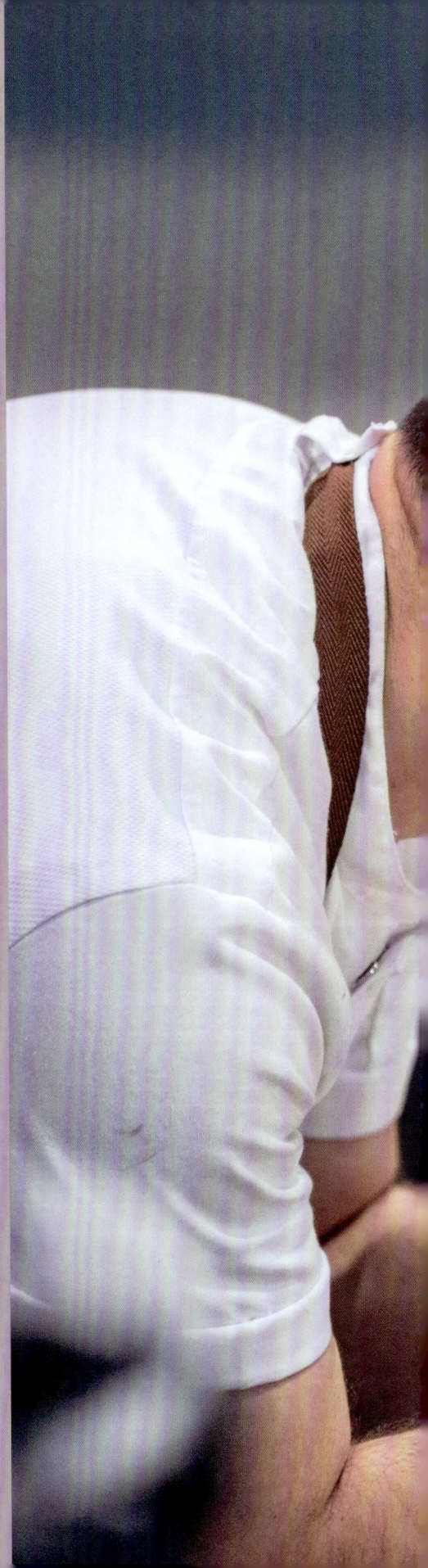

The Great Hall is synonymous with the floating candles that hover above the tables. Originally, these were intended to be a practical effect in the films, with 370 candles suspended by wires ten to fifteen feet above the actors' heads. However, special effects were used on screen, after the real candles' flames were either blown out by the wind or the wires burned through, causing the candles to fall. There is no digital trickery with Jordan's candle desserts—just delicious ingredients. His version consists of orange white chocolate whipped ganache, cranberry gel, candied cranberries, almond streusel, blood orange pearls, and white chocolate snow. Jordan says: "We couldn't be in the Great Hall without having floating candles. The edible ones are a celebration of Christmas flavors, which we imagine the students would enjoy at the Yule Ball."

Zoë's realistic-looking turkey and gravy cake recalls the Christmas dinner enjoyed by Harry, Ron, and Hermione in the *Harry Potter and the Chamber of Secrets* movie. Her dessert contains gingerbread cake, homemade eggnog and cream cheese buttercream, and gingersnap crunch, served with caramel gravy. She explains, "It's a tradition in my family to make eggnog for any big family gathering." Zoë also wanted to use her artistic skills to incorporate a trompe-l'oeil effect, where a 2-D image tricks the eye into thinking it's looking at a 3-D space.

THE SKY'S THE LIMIT

With the trophy in touching distance, the final task was arguably the most complicated for the two remaining *Wizards of Baking* teams. It might not have involved a duel with Lord Voldemort, which Harry had to endure during his final challenge in the Triwizard Tournament, but it did require the chefs to create a six-foot-tall dessert that featured a magical element.

Jordan (left) was inspired by the Christmas dinner scene in the *Harry Potter and the Chamber of Secrets* film, when snow is seen falling inside the building. It's one of several different skies seen in the Great Hall. Fortunately for the diners, they are seen enjoying their food, without being covered in frosty flakes. That special effect was created by digital artists, with the wintry weather fading away midair. Requiring a more practical approach for his dessert, Jordan used tapioca maltodextrin and white chocolate to create his snow.

For her magical technique, Zoë (below left) created a sweet gravy for her Christmas dinner, incorporating flambéed caramel. Elizabeth (above right) made chocolate rocks using liquid nitrogen and foam with an iSi food whipper. Her teammate Juan (below right) opted for mirror glaze and spherification to give the finishing touch to Professor Umbridge's Educational Decrees.

ETERNAL GLORY AWAITS THE WINNERS!

Additional challenges faced by the chefs included a lack of preparation time compared with the previous five tasks. They also had to present their desserts in front of an invited audience, excitedly perched on the Great Hall benches. Ultimately, the moment came when the two teams' final creations were sampled by the *Wizards of Baking* judges.

With the four chefs on tenterhooks, the winners were announced—Zoë and Jordan were crowned as champions and awarded the trophy. "It literally played out like a dream sequence when they announced that we had won," admits Zoë. "It was very strange—it was like I was watching myself! When you get to the final and you're standing there, there is suddenly the realization of all that work you've done. You need time to process that."

"When they were about to announce the winners, my heart was beating so fast," adds Jordan. "I thought I was going to pass out! I don't feel like I ever get nervous, but I really felt it then. When they called our names, I couldn't breathe. We walked up and grabbed the trophy and all the emotion that was in my body just came out. Looking at Zoë, I was even more grateful that we had met each other, especially with what we achieved in the last episode. To be up there in the Great Hall, it's like you're in a different world. It took a while for me to come down from that. I'm extremely grateful and I still can't believe it!"

Zoë's Gingerbread and Eggnog Cake

From *Wizards of Baking*, Episode 6: The Great Hall

For the Cake

3 cups (385 g) all-purpose flour

1½ teaspoons baking powder

½ teaspoon baking soda

1½ tablespoons ground ginger

4 teaspoons ground cinnamon

1 teaspoon ground nutmeg

½ teaspoon ground allspice

¼ teaspoon ground cloves

½ teaspoon salt

¾ cup (170 g) unsalted butter

¾ cup (170 g) light brown sugar, packed

½ cup (100 g) superfine sugar

4 large eggs, at room temperature

1 teaspoon vanilla bean paste

¼ cup (60g) sour cream, at room temperature

1 cup (240 ml) buttermilk, at room temperature

1 cup (240 ml) molasses

For the Homemade Eggnog

1¾ cups (420 ml) whole milk

½ cup and 1 tablespoon (135 ml) heavy cream

1 cinnamon stick

1 vanilla bean or 1 tablespoon vanilla bean paste

1 teaspoon freshly grated nutmeg

3 large eggs, separated

⅓ cup (80 g) superfine cane sugar

7 tablespoons (105 ml) dark rum or bourbon

For the Eggnog Buttercream

¼ cup (35 g) all-purpose flour

1¼ cups (300 ml) homemade eggnog

1 cup plus 1 tablespoon (250 g) unsalted butter

1 cup (225 g) superfine cane sugar

Ground cinnamon

Freshly grated nutmeg

Dark rum to taste (optional)

Zoë's amazing showpiece might have looked like a traditional roast dinner, but it surprised the judges with other fabulous festive flavors. Gingerbread, eggnog buttercream, and gingersnaps combine to create a classic Christmas-themed cake.

TO MAKE THE CAKE

1. Preheat the oven to 350°F (180°C). Prepare three 8-inch round cake pans by greasing the base and sides and lining with parchment paper.

2. Whisk together the flour, baking powder, baking soda, spices, and salt in a bowl. In the bowl of a stand mixer, cream together the butter and sugars until light and fluffy. Add the eggs one at a time, scraping the sides of the bowl each time. Add the vanilla. In a cup with a spout, whisk together the sour cream, buttermilk, and molasses. With the stand mixer running, add half of the dry ingredients followed by half of the wet ingredients. Scrape the sides of the bowl and repeat until the batter is fully combined. Divide the batter evenly among the prepared cake pans and bake for 25 minutes, or until a skewer inserted into the center comes out clean. Place on wire racks to cool.

TO MAKE THE EGGNOG

1. In a saucepan, combine the milk, cream, cinnamon, vanilla, and nutmeg. Bring to a boil over medium heat, then remove from the heat and allow to steep. Remove the cinnamon stick and vanilla bean.

2. In a large bowl or stand mixer, beat the egg yolks and superfine sugar until combined and thick ribbons form when the whisk is lifted. Slowly whisk in the milk mixture and continue to whisk until the mixture is combined and smooth. Add the rum and stir to combine. Refrigerate overnight or for up to 3 days.

3. Before serving, beat the egg whites in a large bowl or stand mixer until soft peaks form. Gently fold into the eggnog until combined. As well as being used in the buttercream, the eggnog can also be enjoyed as a drink, garnished with freshly grated nutmeg.

TO MAKE THE BUTTERCREAM

1. In a pan over medium heat, whisk together the flour and ¾ cup (180 ml) of the eggnog until the mixture thickens. Leave to cool. In a stand mixer, cream together the butter and superfine sugar until light and fluffy (at least 8 minutes). Slowly add the cooled flour and eggnog mixture, one scoop at a time, and beat until well combined and fluffy. Taste and at this point tweak the flavor by adding extra eggnog, cinnamon, and nutmeg. A couple of tablespoons of dark rum can also be added for an extra boozy kick, although remember that the eggnog is already flavored with it!

For the Gingersnap Crunch

2¼ cups (290 g) all-purpose flour

1 teaspoon baking soda

1 teaspoon salt

4 teaspoons ground ginger

1 teaspoon ground cinnamon

½ teaspoon ground cardamom

1 cup (225 g) unsalted butter, softened

½ cup (100 g) light or dark brown sugar, packed

1 cup (200 g) superfine caster sugar

3 tablespoons molasses

1 teaspoon vanilla bean paste

1 large egg

Turbinado or demerara sugar, for rolling

Prep time: 2 hours,
plus cooling and chilling time

Cook time: 30 minutes

TO MAKE THE GINGERSNAP CRUNCH

1. Preheat the oven to 350°F (180°C). Line a baking sheet with parchment paper.

2. In a large bowl, whisk together the flour, baking soda, salt, ginger, cinnamon, and cardamom. Using a stand mixer with the paddle attachment, cream together the butter, brown sugar, superfine sugar, molasses, and vanilla until light and creamy. Beat in the egg.

3. Fold in the flour mixture to the wet ingredients until a dough forms. Use an ice cream scoop to scoop out balls of dough and then roll them in the turbinado sugar.

4. Place the gingersnaps on the prepared baking sheet and bake for 17 to 19 minutes to make sure they are extra crunchy. Allow to cool, place in a ziplock bag, and bash with a rolling pin to create broken chunks.

TO ASSEMBLE THE CAKE

1. When the cakes are cool, trim off any domed tops. If you have any eggnog remaining (you should from the original eggnog recipe), brush each cake layer with it. Add a layer of eggnog buttercream and sprinkle generously with the broken ginger snaps. Repeat. Decorate the top of the cake with piped eggnog buttercream swirls and the gingersnap crunch.

CAKE INSPIRATION!

Although these recipes can be made by hand, Zoë says it is a lot easier to use a stand mixer, or electric beaters at the very least!

Great Hall Floating Candle Cake

Inspired by Zoë and Jordan, Episode 6: The Great Hall

For the Cakes

1 cup (225 g) unsalted butter

1½ cups (300 g) light brown sugar, packed

1½ cups (300 g) granulated sugar

4 large eggs

1 tablespoon vanilla extract

2 cups (200 g) cocoa powder

3 cups (375 g) all-purpose flour

4 teaspoons baking powder

½ teaspoon salt

1⅓ cups (320 g) sour cream

2 cups (480 ml) hot coffee

For the Filling

2 cups (250 g) chopped pecans

2 teaspoons vegetable oil

2 tablespoons sugar

For the Frosting

6 egg whites

¼ teaspoon salt

2 cups (400 g) dark brown sugar, packed

1 cup (240 ml) water

1 teaspoon fresh lemon juice

3 cups (675 g) unsalted butter, cut into tablespoons, plus more for greasing

2 teaspoons vanilla extract

2 cups (340 g) chocolate chips

For Assembly

1 blanched almond

Special Equipment

3 wooden skewers

2 pastry bags

1 large writing tip (about #8)

1 medium writing tip (about #4)

Prep time: 2 hours, plus cooling and chilling time

Cook time: 40 minutes

The Great Hall at Hogwarts is filled with light—a blazing fireplace, glowing flambeaux, and candles that float above the room, illuminating every feast and celebration. This chocolate cake, with a chocolate ganache filling and brown butter frosting, "burns" by a blanched almond wick to light up your dessert table.

TO MAKE THE CAKES

1. Preheat the oven to 350°F (180°C). Line three 6-inch cake pans with rounds of parchment paper fitted in the bottom.

2. In the bowl of a stand mixer fitted with the paddle attachment, cream together the butter, brown sugar, and granulated sugar on medium-high speed until light and fluffy (about 3 minutes). Add the eggs and vanilla. Beat again until well combined. Add the cocoa powder and mix again until completely incorporated.

3. In a small bowl, mix together the flour, baking powder, and salt.

4. Add half of the flour mixture to the butter mixture and mix until incorporated. Scrape down the sides of the bowl and add the sour cream. Mix until incorporated. Add the remaining flour mixture, mix again, and scrape down the sides of the bowl.

5. With the mixer running on low speed, slowly drizzle in the hot coffee. Continue to mix until all of the coffee is incorporated and the batter is smooth, 2 to 3 minutes.

6. Divide the batter among the prepared cake pans and bake for 25 to 30 minutes, or until a cake tester inserted into the center comes out clean. Allow the cakes to cool in the pans for 15 minutes before inverting onto a wire rack and removing the parchment. Let the cakes cool completely on the wire rack.

7. Cut the dome tops off two of the three cakes, and cut each cake into two even layers. Discard the cake scraps or reserve for future use. Place the layers in an airtight container between layers of parchment and freeze while you make the filling and frosting.

TO MAKE THE FILLING

1. Heat a medium skillet over medium-high heat for 1 minute. Add the pecans and toast, stirring continuously, for 1 minute. Turn the heat down to medium-low and add the oil and sugar. Continue stirring until most of the sugar dissolves. Transfer the pecans to a plate and allow to cool completely.

TO ASSEMBLE THE CAKE

1. On a cake stand or small cake round, spread a bit of the chocolate buttercream and place the first layer on top. Put ½ cup (120 g) of the chocolate buttercream over the top of this first layer and smooth with an offset spatula. Sprinkle with ¼ cup (35 g) of the pecan filling. Repeat these steps with the next four layers and then top with the sixth layer. Use any remaining chocolate frosting to seal the edges of the layers. Press three skewers, evenly placed, through the top layer all the way to the bottom, trimming off any excess skewers. This will ensure that this extra-tall cake stays stable. Refrigerate for 30 minutes.

2. Remove the cake from the refrigerator, and use an offset spatula to frost the top and sides of the cake with the buttercream. Smooth the sides, and create a low point in the middle of the top by pushing frosting toward the edges. Place about 1 cup (225 g) of frosting in a pastry bag fitted with a large writing tip and pipe the "melted" rim of the candle. Use the offset spatula to smooth and sculpt this, disguising the piping and creating a wax look. Chill the cake for another 30 minutes.

3. Gently heat about 1 cup (225 g) of frosting in the microwave, for 5 to 10 seconds only. Load this frosting into a pastry bag fitted with a medium writing tip. Remove the cake from the refrigerator and use the frosting to create the "wax drips." The cold cake will stop the drips as they slide down, making the candle effect.

4. Refrigerate until an hour before serving, then remove and allow to come to room temperature. Place the blanched almond as the wick in the center of the cake. The almond will light briefly if desired.

5. The best way to cut this extra-tall cake is to cut halfway down from the top and then cut in from the side, removing slices that are three layers tall. Once the top has been served, the bottom three layers can be cut as usual.

TO MAKE THE FROSTING

1. Add the egg whites and salt to the bowl of a stand mixer fitted with a whisk attachment. In a medium heavy-bottomed saucepan over medium-high heat, combine the brown sugar and water and bring to a boil. Whisk the egg whites until frothy, about 1 minute. Add the lemon juice and whisk until soft peaks form, 2 to 3 minutes more, then shut off the mixer.

2. Grease a heatproof 4-cup measuring cup with butter and set aside. Fit the saucepan with a candy thermometer and, when the sugar mixture reaches 238°F (114°C), pour it into the measuring cup.

3. Slowly add the sugar syrup to the egg whites in small batches, whisking after each addition. When all the syrup is added, beat the mixture on high speed for 3 to 5 minutes, until the meringue is completely cool (the outside of the bowl should be cool to the touch).

4. Add the butter, one to two pieces at a time, beating well on medium speed after each addition. Once all the butter has been incorporated, add the vanilla and briefly beat on high speed until smooth.

5. In a medium microwave-safe bowl, add the chocolate chips. Heat for 1 minute and then let stand for 5 minutes. Stir until smooth, allow to cool for 1 to 2 minutes, and then stir into 3 cups (675 g) of the buttercream.

ZOË AND JORDAN
IN THEIR OWN WORDS

On the first day of filming, eighteen immensely talented chefs began an extraordinary baking challenge at the Harry Potter Studio Tour, Leavesden, UK. As the final episode ended, cake artist Zoë Burmester and executive pastry chef Jordan Pilarski were proclaimed winners. Their spectacular culinary creations included the interior of Gringotts Bank, books from Flourish and Blotts, and a tea party inspired by Dolores Umbridge. Here, the *Wizards of Baking* winners reminisce about their experiences in the competition.

Congratulations on being the winning team. How did it feel to be presenting Harry Potter–inspired desserts at these famous studios?

Zoë: The whole situation was incredibly surreal! We were filming through the night because the Studios are open to the public during the day. Wheeling these massive, intricate showpieces through the sets in the dead of night was a dreamlike situation. I genuinely felt as though I had been transported into this parallel world. And then on top of that, each time you go through a judging, it is very draining emotionally. But both of us were always aware how cool it was to be presenting our work on the sets—we felt like we were in the films. What an opportunity! That was not lost on us. I don't think it was lost on any of the competitors.

Jordan: You're already thinking, "I just flew across the world to film this!" You might have some idea of what the Studios are going to look like, and it's not even close. It blows it out of the water! Like Zoë was saying, the logistics between just making things, transporting them, going through the sets … there's no way anybody could have thought about that, but it's just so cool. There were times when Zoë and I had to just stop and take in the moment. We could not believe the opportunity that we had to go through this whole process. You may think, "Oh, it's just a baking show," but you're in a whole different world.

Where did the food preparation take place?

Zoë: A huge kitchen was built for us in one of the adjacent studio set stages. That is where we baked and created the cakes. There was a whole military operation behind the scenes to get these cakes from the kitchen studio set to the Harry Potter set!

Jordan: We had to transport the finished showpiece from the kitchen to vans that took us to the Harry Potter sets. The culinary team was amazing and figured out the timings and had contingencies if it rained. One day, it was raining, so the team carried a canopy over this 150-pound build. It was the most planned out I've ever seen, just because we had to transport these massive builds.

Zoë: Any cake-maker will tell you that traveling with a cake in a van is the most stressful part of the job! Because these are sacred sets, there were naturally limitations to what we could do. In the normal world, you might do things like airbrushing last minute. Here, there were certain conditions, so you couldn't use open flames or airbrush … we had to think ahead. Sometimes you will assemble something after transportation because it makes sense, but we couldn't necessarily do that in the Studios. Those added elements made it sort of spicier, I suppose!

Jordan: For the second challenge, we were dropped off at the back of Platform 9¾ and had to go all the way to the Gringotts set, which is a thirty-minute walk. I remember that was stressful. It was a long, exhausting day because we had already baked for eight hours.

Zoë: And then, after all that, you had to be judged!

For the Diagon Alley episode, you had the additional challenge of having to market your cakes to Harry Potter fans at the studio.

Jordan: We had to set up shop and feed fifty people and it was probably midnight or 1:00 a.m. We just went through a long day prepping and creating, but then you've got to put on a face and be like, "Hey, come and enjoy this!" They were the biggest Harry Potter fans, so there was no time to be exhausted—we needed to be on our A game and be able to articulate and sell our books to these super fans. It was fun, too. We were around the cast for so long, and then you get fifty people from the outside world that you can talk to. That helped in that situation, because it was exciting.

Zoë: We had to make fifty of the cakes, which suggested there would be fifty people to eat them! But we were so focused in the kitchen, it was only when we arrived on set that the reality of what we had to do sunk in. We had to pitch our wares! Like Jordan said, you had to pivot mentally from a very focused, timed challenge to putting your public face on. But I really like connecting with people, and once I got over the shock of what we had to do, I actually found it very energizing meeting all the fans. It was also the only challenge where we were all together as competitors. The production team kept us on our toes, as we never really knew the format of every show as it happened. Quite a lot of times, you were operating without knowing what the competitors were doing, but on this challenge, we were together.

Does that mean you saw most of the cakes for the first time when they were judged?

Zoë: Sometimes, but not always! It wasn't a situation where all the teams were judged together, side by side. We were judged individually or sometimes as two pairings. Diagon Alley was the only challenge where we got to see what other people had done. In Challenge One, Jordan and I were judged alongside Miko and Chris. So, out of nine cakes in that challenge, we only saw one other. But Jordan and I had the approach from the start to focus solely on our cakes. To that end, we didn't worry too much about what the other teams were doing.

Was there any one dessert that stands out as a particular favorite for you?

Jordan: I think Diagon Alley was my favorite, because that was a challenge that was specifically geared toward the pastry chef, I think, even though Zoë and I did it all together. But there was a lot of process to that dessert. It's just like what I do in my normal job in my normal life. When creating plated desserts, in research and development, you think about it for so long, and when it comes to actually putting it on a plate, that process is really cool. In this episode, I knew exactly how I wanted to do it. I wanted to create something that was amazing and fitting, but also we had to execute it. I think we did a really good job. It's something I'm really proud of.

Zoë: There are a few that stick out. I'm really proud of Challenge Five, because it was such a difficult brief to realize. We also knew what we were up against. We knew that Juan and Elizabeth were doing the phoenix, which is so iconic and arguably a winning brief to begin with! We also knew that Miko and Chris were doing paintings. We had been given Time-Turners as our theme, and that was just hard. I am really proud with what we came up with. We also wanted to play on sherbet lemons and illusion food. I was really happy with the flavors, and I think it looked great in Dumbledore's office.

Did winning the Dumbledore's Office challenge give you a boost going into the final round?

Zoë: Winning Challenge Five gave us a huge boost because we actually hadn't won a challenge up until that point, even though we had come close. And we were up against two fantastic teams, so I wasn't expecting it. We genuinely just did not know which way that was going to go. It helped us decide how we were going to approach Challenge Six. That final round is the culmination of our journey on the show: what we had gone through, what we learned about each other, what we realized was and wasn't going to work, and what we wanted to end our experience on. That's why we chose the themes of Christmas, family, and community. We showcased a lot of different skills between the two of us in Challenge Six. I got to incorporate illusion food and sculpted cakes, which I was happy about, and Jordan did some really beautiful sugar-work all assembled atop some structurally sound chocolate work. For my part, I felt that we really pulled together a strong story with the design of this showpiece, which is the thing that's so important to me in my cake work. It was a fitting way for us to end the experience, whether we had won or not.

The designs are very intricate. Were any of them particularly difficult to realize?

Jordan: For our second challenge, in Gringotts, we decided to do a chandelier made out of sugar. It was a minimalist design that was huge, and it was tough, to say the least.

When it came to how long certain things took, that day was the hardest one. I'm still proud that we did it, but that was a very difficult brief. It was maybe a rude awakening, as it gave us something to think about moving forward on all our other designs. It gave us a pretty realistic approach on what can and can't be done.

Zoë: Things conspired against us. Hot kitchens ... melting sugar ... we were always going to get a challenge like that. It was probably better that we had it earlier in the run than later. I didn't know if we were going to make it through after that challenge. When we did, it felt that if we can survive the melting chandelier, then we're good! We can do this.

Are there any flavor profiles in your desserts that you think worked particularly well?

Jordan: I'll keep going back to the books, but I think about the way that the flavors in the rosemary olive oil cake and the raspberry rose jelly combined together. Zoë really wanted to add those floral notes. I didn't know how it was going to play out, and it actually turned out really well. One judge said it was the best olive oil cake he had ever eaten. That really showcases the relationship that Zoë and I had. I think we were both really happy with the flavor combinations we created.

Zoë: We wanted to introduce some flavors that speak to the bookshop. What do pages taste like? It's a weird one! So we came up with the idea of wood—lemonwood, olivewood, and rosewood. We bounced ideas off each other, like the

sherbet lemons. We wanted something that wasn't a sherbet lemon in terms of flavor profile. I said to Jordan that we have this thing in the UK called a Bakewell tart, which is hugely popular, and is certainly something that Dumbledore himself would eat and love. I'm throwing out things at Jordan that he isn't necessarily familiar with, but then he's taking those ideas and putting his Jordan spin on it.

Did you have any arguments about how to approach the challenges?

Jordan: There are a couple of episodes where I looked at Zoë, saying: "We can't do this." She looked at me and said, "No, we can." She proved me wrong a couple of times throughout the show. Even in the first episode with the Hufflepuff badger, we didn't think we were going to be able to get those things done—and she pulled it out of the hat. It was amazing. I wouldn't say there were arguments, because that's a big word. It was more of an open line of communication, and you have little tiffs or disagreements about what works well and what doesn't. It's just based off the way we think differently. You work through it and come to create amazing things at the end.

Zoë: I remember saying to Jordan the first time we met that I'm going to do and say things that you're not going to like or agree with and that's OK. It's OK if you tell me that. We don't have the luxury of time to spare each other's feelings. We have a common goal here and that's our focus. So even if there are inevitable conflicts of opinion, we have to be grown-ups and place ego to one side. Ultimately, our drive was always to work from a place of trust and to always try to do the right thing by and for the challenge. Whilst Jordan and I share some of the same values, we do work very differently. I'm sure when Jordan first saw me in the kitchen, he was probably thinking, "What have I got myself into?!"

How did you get on with the other chefs?

Jordan: We had plenty of time to get to know them. We had time to decompress when we were on set when waiting for judging. We made jokes, we talked to each other. I don't have anything bad to say about anybody, and we still talk to each other.

Zoë: I really enjoyed getting to know the other contestants. We did bond as a group, and every time a couple left, we all felt it, because we had all experienced the show together, albeit for different lengths of time. The show is something that is going to forever bond us all. Personally, it was really interesting to meet a variety of chefs, learn their varied stories, and hear about their different baking influences. It's a great team of people, and I feel lucky that I was a part of it, honestly.

How did you feel immediately after filming finished on the final episode?

Jordan: When we were able to get back to the hotel room, I sat with my own thoughts for a little bit. It was a good moment for me to take it all in. Then, we had to fly home, and the following day I went back to work. Everybody talks about how hard it is to keep it secret. Work was busy, so that helped, but every now and then I caught myself thinking about it and replayed winning over and over in my head!

Zoë: All the competitors will have been asked whether they won before the show aired. I just said, "Yes, I am in the show, and no, I can't tell you!" I told family members they would enjoy watching it more not knowing. When you know someone who is on a show like this, you are naturally more invested, and I didn't want to detract from that excitement.

Do you have plans to work together again?

Jordan: We made plans to see each other again at the beginning. Zoë said that if we did win, she is coming out to see me. So I'm holding her to that! The relationship that we have gained from this is important. Zoë is an incredible person. She's very creative and amazing at what she does. Also, we got along really well, so I'd love to travel to New York and see what she does day-to-day. I know that my wife would love to meet her, too.

Zoë: I think it's a shame that we don't live closer. If we did, I could definitely see myself knocking on Jordan's door. I think we bring very different skills to the partnership, but we're very similar with how we approach things, and that always makes for a successful partnership in whatever you do. I would definitely work with Jordan again. I literally couldn't think of anything better in the world than to write a cookbook with him.

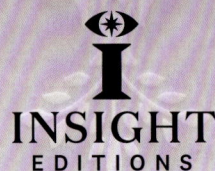

I

INSIGHT
EDITIONS

PO Box 3088—San Rafael, CA 94912
www.insighteditions.com

Find us on Facebook: www.facebook.com/InsightEditions
Follow us on Instagram: @insighteditions

WB *Harry Potter*

ISBN: 979-8-88663-904-9

Publisher: Raoul Goff
VP, Co-Publisher: Vanessa Lopez
Creative Director: Stella Bradley
Product Designer: Paul Montague
Sourcing Director: Tracey Hinchliffe
Subsidiary Rights: Lina s Palma-Temena
VP, Manufacturing: Alix Nicholaeff
Managing Editor: Mary Beth Garhart
Copy Editor: Karen Levy
Editorial Assistant: Lia Sina

Apple Crumble and Custard Cake (p.36), Chocolate Whiskey Cake (p.54), Gingerbread and Eggnog Cake (p.126): Recipes by Zoë Burmester; Abuelita Spice Chocolate Crémeux (p.37), Rosemary and Thyme Olive Oil Cake (p.69), Blackcurrant Macarons and Earl Grey Crêpe Cake (p.84), Ginger Cake (p.106): Recipes by Jordan Pilarski; Chocolate Shortbread Wands (p.38), Elderflower Potion Bottle Cake (p.40), Champagne and Raspberry Money Bag Cake (p.56), Olive Oil, Rosemary, Lemon, and Thyme Book Cakes (p.66), Wand Box Cakes (p.72), Bakewell Pots with Lemony White Chocolate (p.108): Recipes by Gabriella English; Jam Pastry Acceptance Letters (p.42), Hagrid's "Happee Birthdae" Cupcakes (p.44), Quality Quidditch Cake Pops (p.70), Patronus Cake (p.88), Mandrake Cry Cupcakes (p.92): Recipes by Elena P. Craig, first featured in *Harry Potter Feasts & Festivities: An Official Book of Magical Celebrations, Crafts, and Party Food Inspired by the Wizarding World* (© Insight Editions, 2022); Skull Cakes (p.86): Recipe by Sarah Walker Caron and Elena P. Craig, first featured in *Harry Potter and Fantastic Beasts: Official Wizarding Cookbook* (© Insight Editions, 2024); Great Hall Floating Candle Cake (p.128): Recipe by Elena P. Craig, first featured in *Harry Potter: Official Christmas Cookbook* (© Insight Editions, 2023).

The publishers would like to thank Morgan Hass, Nikki Scott,
and Lauren Mueller for their help in the making of this book.

ROOTS of PEACE   🌳 REPLANTED PAPER

Insight Editions, in association with Roots of Peace, will plant two trees for each tree used in the manufacturing of this book. Roots of Peace is an internationally renowned humanitarian organization dedicated to eradicating land mines worldwide and converting war-torn lands into productive farms and wildlife habitats. Roots of Peace will plant two million fruit and nut trees in Afghanistan and provide farmers there with the skills and support necessary for sustainable land use.

Manufactured in China by Insight Editions

10 9 8 7 6 5 4 3 2 1